W9-BSE-574

CL
Worship

MY HEART'S DESIRE

LIVING EVERY MOMENT
in the WONDER *of* WORSHIP

DAVID JEREMIAH

INTEGRITY®
PUBLISHERS
Nashville

MY HEART'S DESIRE

By David Jeremiah
Copyright © 2002 by David Jeremiah.
Published by Integrity Publishers, a Division of Integrity Media, Inc.
5250 Virginia Way, Suite 110, Brentwood, TN 37027.

Published in association with Yates & Yates,
LLP, Literary Agents, Orange, California.

Unless otherwise indicated,
Scripture quotations used in this book are from
The New King James Version, copyright © 1979, 1980, 1982,
Thomas Nelson, Inc., Publishers.

Other Scripture references are from the following sources:
The Holy Bible, New Century Version (NCV),
Copyright © 1987, 1988, 1991 by W Publishing Group,
Nashville, Tennessee 37214. Used by permission.

The King James Version of the Bible (KJV).

Cover Design: The Office of Bill Chiaravalle
www.officeofbc.com
Interior Design: Inside Out Design & Typesetting

Library of Congress Cataloging-in-Publication Data

Jeremiah, David.
   My heart's desire: living every moment in the wonder of worship / David
Jeremiah: edited by Rob Suggs.
      p. cm.
   ISBN 1-59145-000-4
   1. Christian life—Baptist authors.   2. Worship.   I. Suggs, Rob.   II. Title.
BV4501.3 .J47   2002
248.3—dc21

                                                            2002068543

Printed in the United States of America
02 03 04 05 06 BVG 9 8 7 6 5 4 3 2

CONTENTS

~ DEDICATION ~

To my Lord and Savior, Jesus Christ,
Who alone is worthy to receive
glory and honor and power and riches
and wisdom and strength and blessing—
to Him who sits on the throne, and
to the Lamb, forever and ever!

—REVELATION 4–5

~AKNOWLEDGMENTS~

A S THIS BOOK IS BEING RELEASED, Donna and I have just finished twenty years of ministry at Shadow Mountain Community Church. These have been wonderful years of serving our Lord and ministering to a gracious congregation. Each Sunday as our church gathers I am filled with a sense of expectation as I anticipate our time of corporate worship. Over the years we have experienced some awesome moments of wonder as we have sensed the presence of the Lord in our midst. Worshiping God as a body of believers is one of the special privileges He has granted to His children.

But this book is not primarily about congregational worship. *My Heart's Desire* is about personal worship . . . one-on-one worship with Almighty God. Worship was never meant to be a Sunday-only experience. God is not seeking for churches to worship Him, He is seeking for individuals to worship Him. As worshiping God becomes our everyday lifestyle experience, we discover that our times together with the family of God take on deeper meaning. In other words, worship is not a one-hour experience once a week! Worship is a moment-by-moment relationship with God that lasts all week long.

I am still growing in my understanding of what it means to live every moment in the wonder of worship. I am so very thankful for those who have helped shape my thinking. Steve and Susan Caudill joined our ministry staff over a decade ago. Together they have led us in worshiping God each Sunday. We have spent many hours talking about worship and seeking with all our hearts to lead our people into God's presence on the Lord's Day. Thank you, Steve and Susan, for your commitment to excellence, your faithfulness to God, and your desire to make worship the heart's desire of each one of us.

Rob Suggs is the writer–editor who helps make my thoughts come to life. He understands my heart and is able to take my words and make them crisper and brighter. I always look forward to working with Rob, and I trust we shall be able to be partners for many books to come!

Sealy Yates and I have been great friends for many years and almost a dozen books. As my literary agent, he represents me to our publishers and regularly mentions my name before the Lord. He cares about me and the work that God has called me to do. Every pastor needs someone like Sealy in his life!

As my administrative assistant, Carrie Mann has managed the many phone conferences and meetings that helped bring this project to completion. Dianne Stark and Barbara Boucher read the manuscript and made valuable suggestions. Helen Barnhart was of great assistance in locating bibliographical references. Thanks, ladies, for your diligent help!

I would also like to express my appreciation to Joey Paul and Byron Williamson for encouraging me to put my thoughts on worship into writing. Throughout this entire project we have had many hours of interaction about *My Heart's Desire,* and I have loved the sense of team-work. Thank you, Joey and Byron, for allowing me to write one of the first books published by Integrity.

Finally I want to express my deepest appreciation to my wife Donna. Without her encouragement, I would never have written the first book. Our partnership in all that God has done and is doing in our lives is one of my greatest treasures. Together we are praying that God will use *My Heart's Desire* to bring blessing to many lives and glory to our Savior's name!

—DAVID JEREMIAH
San Diego, California

1

A View from a Throne

ONE

A View from a Throne

OUR HEARTS ARE POUNDING as the great doors swing open before us—the doors where earth is left behind and heaven begins. Almost feverish with anticipation, you and I step into the great room, and we're immediately and completely overcome by all that lies before our senses.

No eye has seen a room of such sparkling magnificence; no ear has heard such music. There is no art or edifice in the mortal world that could have prepared us for this. We can't speak or even allow our world-weakened eyes to wonder at the glories that fill the throne room of the King of creation. Without our even realizing it, great tears are streaming down our cheeks.

The ceiling of the room is too high to be seen; it rises majestically to the farthest reaches of infinity. The walls gleam with a living tapestry of the King's mighty works through the ages. And the angels surround us as embodiments of light and song, lifting up praises to the Name that is above all names. The very air we breathe has the sweet taste of paradise and intense joy that is beyond description. But all these things only lead our eyes to the throne, for the King Himself is there.

Our eyes are inadequate to take in His glory, of course. But we do gaze upon His hand, the hand that shaped the contours of every planet and flung every star into space, the hand that brought light from darkness and order from chaos. Something rustles in His hand: an ageless document. The scroll glows with the light of wisdom and providence, and it is sealed not once, but seven times. Here in our Father's hand is the title deed to earth.

The biblical Book of Revelation describes this scroll and its procession of seals. Through the chapters of that book, the seals are unfastened one by one as the final business of time, the final details of God's plan, come to final fruition. Judgment and wrath lie in the unfastening of these seals; redemption and victory, too. As each seal is removed, every question finds its solution. Every riddle is forever solved. And for that reason, the eyes of hundreds of millions of souls watch intently.

Did I mention the hundreds of millions? This room, of course, lies outside the created realms of time and space. History and proximity are irrelevant here. That's why the throng stands with us in this room. From every land and every epoch of history, they have come to see the final decree of destiny at the throne.

But there is one soul who has stepped forward, and we know in an instant who he is: John the Apostle, transported through a vision on the island of Patmos. He is here to observe and to record the prophecies that will become the final book of the Bible, the one we call Revelation. John is the messenger, the reporter. He, you, I, and all the countless throng of witnesses, are standing in the scene recorded in that book's fifth chapter.

And now, an angel comes before us. He cries out, in a powerful voice, a message for the assembled throng. "Who is worthy to open the scroll," he asks, "and to loose its seals?" Is it our imaginations or does the great throng, in one motion, step sadly backward? With the angel's question, all eyes are lowered to the floor. A spirit of mournful gloom can be felt for the first time, for no one counts himself worthy to accept the invitation to unfasten those seals. We find that, just like Jesus' beloved friend John, we are weeping aloud. We've been reminded of the things we'd rather not consider—the stains and blemishes that make us unfit to know the unspeakable joy of perfect fellowship with the Father.

Here in this scroll, the one we dare not touch, lies the final plan by which Jesus will have ultimate dominion over the earth. Here is the picture of a world with Jesus as the King of kings and the Lord of lords. Here is the judgment to be poured, finally and irrevocably, upon the evil ones who have rejected Him. How can we not be eager for the unfolding of such a document? Is no one worthy to step forward and open that scroll? We continue to weep bitterly. In the next moment, we will hear a voice of comfort from over our shoulders. As we'll see, our tears can be dried, for there is hope.

Later on our journey, we'll return to this room one more time for the rest of the story. We'll find out who can open the scroll and what the implications are for you and for me. But for now, let's freeze that scene in our minds—the scene of the beautiful throne room where the Father sits and where He beckons us to step forward and take part in the great adventure. No matter how unworthy we may be, He looks upon us, smiles, and urges us to come and help Him carry out His great plan for this world. And we can only look at our feet. We can only step away uncomfortably and feel so many regrets.

Can you identify with that scenario? It may be symbolized in a book of complex and intense future prophecy, but I believe it's a picture of the life too many of us lead every day. We all feel the void in our hearts and the invitation to go deeper with God, to come more boldly into His presence. We want to worship, as Jesus said, in spirit and in truth. We want that joy and exhilaration. We long to identify with the Lordship of Christ over this world with all its problems and all its darkness.

So what prevents us from leaping forward and running into His arms? What holds us back from worshiping and praising Him in the midst of life?

In this book I hope you and I can thoroughly explore the answer to that question. If you've always longed to know God better, to worship Him with all your heart, to experience His presence regardless of life's circumstances, I hope this book will point you farther down the path to that kind of life. If you're new to the kingdom of God, my prayer is that this book will be your primer in taking those first steps toward a lifestyle of worship. If you're older and wiser in the spiritual realities, I hope this book will revive the first joy and eagerness for God's face that you may have lost over the years. And if, like so many of us, you're somewhere in-between—our journey is certain to give you a new and fresh understanding of what it means to come before God every day with a heart filled with praise.

So prepare for a journey of faith, discovery, and wonder. It will take us to many destinations, from the worship service to the workplace, from the earthly to the eternal. Not least of all, I hope it will bring you to a new encounter with yourself, your motives, and your potential as a child of God. Are you ready? Let's depart now with open eyes and an eager spirit, so when we do return to that room where earth gives way to eternity, there will be nothing but joy as we gaze into the Father's eyes. There will be no weeping, only laughter. And as He invites us to come forward, we'll be prepared to rejoice in the thing we were all created to do—to know and to love God as He has first loved us.

2

Do You Ever Wonder?

TWO

⤳ *Do You Ever Wonder?* ⤳

THE AMERICAN SPACE PROGRAM launched our imaginations when men first landed on the moon. Do you remember? One story of the space program's fascination happened during the last days of our Apollo flights. Jacob Needleman was one of the reporters gathered to cover the launch of Apollo 17 in 1975.

The launch was scheduled for evening, and the reporters were making a social occasion out of it. They strolled the lawn of the press section, where refreshments were laid out on picnic tables. They snacked, drank, and cracked their usual jokes drenched in sarcasm. That's the way of reporters, who see and report the worst of the world's events on a daily basis.

Finally it was time for the great Atlas rocket, a thirty-five-story tower of power, to hurtle into the heavens. There was the familiar countdown, then the launch. As Needleman tells the story in Bill Moyers's book *A World of Ideas II,* the reporters were suddenly all but blinded by a vast field of orange light. Their eyes could barely handle the intensity. Then, in deafening silence—given that sound travels less rapidly than light—the great rocket thundered into the dark canopy of night. The sound waves arrived seconds later in full force with a cataclysmic *whooooooooosh* and a mighty *hummmmmm* that jangled the reporters' bones. They felt their toes tremble with the earth.

The rocket traveled higher, then higher still as the first stage ignited in spectacular blue flame. It seemed to have become a star, bearing three men bound for glory. And then all of it was gone, vanished into the periphery of the atmosphere and the depths of space. There was silence among the press corps. The interrupted wisecracks died on the reporters' lips, not to be recalled. Needleman saw the men's eyes filled with light, their mouths wide open, their faces lit by the inner glow of sheer wonder.

Most amazing of all was the sight of hardened cynical newspapermen whose whole bearing seemed changed. The edge had been knocked off; smiles were now authentic and gentle. Conversation was quiet and reverent. Men were helping each other with their chairs and notebooks. If only for a moment in time, a sense of awe had taken possession of them and changed their behavior patterns.[1]

Such moments are all too few in the dark night of these times. In a true age of wonders filled by spaceships, the Internet, and microchips—all amazing inventions our grandparents could never have foretold—we have become a generation characterized not by awe, but by cynicism and empty nihilism. That in itself is a wonder; for how can we, who have seen so many new marvels, find ourselves so spiritually empty and incapable of wonder?

I wonder . . .

Do You Ever Wonder?

Our preceding century began with predictions of a future utopia just around the corner. The victories of science and industry would surely deliver new prosperity, new capabilities, and new answers to old problems. Even the First World War was labeled "The War to End All Wars" and popularly seen as a more civilized world's final conflict. The twentieth century arrived with the marvel of the light bulb, but it left with the explosion of mass destruction.

Somewhere along the way, we discovered that utopia is elusive. Wars became more ghastly; technology was turned not just to cures, but to new, man-created crises. The transitional moment between the "Century of Progress" and whatever lies in the new millennium came on September 11, 2001. Two of the world's most magnificent towers, symbols of sophistication and free-world commerce, were savaged by the forces of primitive hatred. As we watched images of people leaping to their deaths and heard of the thousands who perished in collapsing steel and mortar, we felt anything but wonder. We were chilled by horror and dread beyond anything we might have considered before. We wondered if we could ever live again without looking over our shoulders.

Many of us live in cities where sunsets and mountain horizons have become distant memories. The majestic stars are blocked out by the smoky mists of industry. Just as our capabilities have grown exponentially, our capacity for wonder seems to have withered. A century ago, G. K. Chesterton wrote, "The world is not lacking in wonders, but in a sense of wonder."

Before we can say anything about worship, we must come to grips with this idea of wonder. For worship can never be the sole work of the rational mind. It can't be drawn up on paper or measured out by charts. Worship and wonder, which are so closely connected, are all about coming to the end of our measurements. In the presence of Almighty God, as the apostle John discovered, the sense of wonder comes naturally and leaves us changed. How could we respond any other way? But without the capability of awe, where we stand at the edge of ourselves and gaze beyond, we will never come into His presence.

This book is about living *every moment* in the wonder of worship. I want us to be able to sweep aside the complexity and despair of our time, if only for those brief moments when we attend to these chapters. Then I want us to take a deep breath and remember what it's like to be a child with wide eyes, taking in something greater and more *wonder*ful than any sight we've seen before. What was it for you? Christmas morning at the age of five? An electric train that filled an entire room? Your first sight of the ocean? I want us to discover that in the presence of God, available wherever we are and whenever we choose, we can live in the essence of that awe. We can be like those reporters, our cynicism melted away by the light that comes from another world.

Do you ever wonder? How long has it been since you've been a child again, gaping with wide eyes? How would it change your life if you could live like that every day? How would it change the people around you?

I hope you're already sensing it—your heart's very desire. This is what has been lacking in so many lives. We've wandered through the emptiness when we could have been wondering at the fullness of the love of God. Your heart's desire, even if you haven't come to realize it, is to live every moment in the wonder of worship.

Do You Ever Wonder?

From Genesis to Revelation

Recorded history begins with sheer wonder. It ends in the same way. And what do you think constitutes the center? Yes, the entire Bible is structured around humanity standing amazed in the presence of God. Let's take a look.

Genesis begins, as everyone knows, with the creation of the world. None of us was there to witness it, but we're given the account of how God fashioned the heavens and the earth with His powerful hand. Through writing inspired by the Spirit of God, we can stand and behold the moment when God said, "Let there be light"; when He divided the waters from the firmament; when He caused the earth to bring forth grass and when He placed the sun, the moon, and the stars in the sky. On each occasion we know that God said, "It is good."

Yes, it is good! That's our most basic response, too, when we look into the star-filled sky or see the sun rise in glory over a mountain, bathing the skies in orange and deep blue. But when we see that which is perfect, that which God has proclaimed *good,* we respond also with our emotions. We stand amazed; we wonder. And that's a point we must stop and consider, for the ability to marvel lies at the very center of our identities as human beings created in the divine image.

Stand before that sunset and not only will your eyes be filled, but also your very soul and imagination. But if your favorite dog is with you, you'll find him sniffing at the ground—perhaps attending to a trouble-some flea. No matter what any contemporary scientist wants to tell you, there's a vast difference between you and a common beast. You marvel. You mourn. You laugh and love. But it's the first of those, the capacity to wonder, that immediately stamps us as God's special children. If we're merely an evolution-driven complex of firing neurons and instinctive stimulus responses, why would we respond *emotionally* to the rising or setting of the sun? Why would we be drawn to music, and what is there in Darwin's system that would make us laugh?

The capacity to wonder is the built-in channel given to us for encountering God Himself. The capacity to wonder is the open doorway to worship. It is the soul given occasion to take stock of true spiritual perspective. Without wonder we could not see. God "crammed earth with heaven," to paraphrase the poet Elizabeth Barrett Browning, because too soon we forget that heaven is in our view. Therefore He fills the earth with heavenly billboards, and if we fail to get the message, there's something dead within us. Albert Einstein put it this way: "The most beautiful thing we can experience is the mysterious. It is the source of all true art and science. He to whom the emotion is a stranger, who can no longer pause to wonder and stand rapt in awe, is as good as dead: his eyes are closed."[2]

A Book Full of Wonder

But what about the rest of the Bible? It's not only a wonderful book, but a book full of wonder. We've seen how it begins, and we've seen, in the preceding chapter, how it ends. We've already stood with John at the threshold of eternity and witnessed something of the culmination of human history, from the perspective of God. Again, we find that it's important to God that we take in this experience vicariously. That's why He gave the vision to John, so that you and I and anyone in possession of the Word of God could marvel at the majesty of the sovereign King upon His throne.

Creation and culmination are the bookends of Scripture. But in the very heart of the book, in its physical center, we find the Book of Psalms. These songs, too, are all about worship and wonder. I can't imagine a believer staying too long out of this book. Consider this song of wonder:

> O LORD, our Lord,
> How excellent is Your name in all the earth,
> You Who have set Your glory above the heavens! . . .
> When I consider Your heavens, the work of Your fingers,
> The moon and the stars, which You have ordained,
> What is man that You are mindful of him,
> And the son of man that You visit him?
> For You have made him a little lower than the angels,
> And You have crowned him with glory and honor.
>
> —PSALMS 8:1, 3-5

It's no wonder that this particular psalm has been a favorite of men and women through the ages. For one thing, it expresses how we all feel at one time or another (hopefully quite often). God has set His glory *above* the heavens. We peer into the sky and we know that, as majestic as the view may be, there is something beyond—something above all that we see and feel. I believe that's the essence of wonder—the "aha" in our awe. That's because God has encompassed creation with His glory.

The night sky casts a divine, pensive spell over us, as people have found through the ages; God designed it to do so. David the psalmist, who gazed out upon those stars during so many nights of watching over his sheep, must have continually marveled. And he must have realized who was watching over him. As he considered his Lord, according to the psalm, he finally was brought to consider himself. "Who am I that I would be worthy of even a thin moment of Your attention?" he wondered.

"I look upon the crown of Your creation, and I wonder: How is it that You could place a crown upon me?" For David, of course, a royal destiny did beckon. But true worship has this effect upon us: It simultaneously humbles and uplifts us. In other words, worship places us exactly where we should be, in the realization that we are small, yet a little lower than the angels; we are tiny creatures in the presence of God, but tiny creatures whom He adores.

The Bible, then, is more than a wonderful book—it's a book full of wonder. It begins with the wonder of creation, implanted deeply within us. It ends with the wonderful culmination of God's final judgment. And in the very center, with the psalms, are songs of praise and wonder. His central written revelation to us is just as crammed with heaven as creation itself. But the challenge is this: We are flawed, fallen creatures, prone to pluck at forbidden fruit rather than bask in worship as God designed us. How do we confront these limitations?

Growing Up to Childlikeness

If we want to worship in spirit and in truth, we need to rediscover the capacity to wonder that God placed within each of us. It has been distorted by sin, so that our perceptions have been twisted. The precise opposite of wonder is cynicism, and I doubt there has ever been a time more characterized by cynicism than this one. If we're not careful, we'll all fall into that trap. After all, cynicism is in the cultural air we breathe every day. Unless you live on a desert island, you spend more time being exposed to cynical attitudes than you do eating or exercising. Think of our television shows. Consider the movies our young people attend and the music that pulses through their earphones.

Do You Ever Wonder?

After September 11, 2001, there was much media discussion of "the death of irony," but in fact little has changed. There is a culture of sarcasm that has for decades filtered down from our media and many of our leaders to infect all of us. I've often said that I don't see how a committed follower of Christ can maintain a sarcastic approach to humor, but we have so few other models before us. After a while, we no longer marvel at Oz, the Great and Powerful—we're straining our necks to find the little shrunken man behind the curtain. We're certain there must always be one, for all seems to be sham and subterfuge. While the preacher is telling us about God, we're wondering how much they pay him to preach the sermon. Cynicism is a deadly infection that eats away our childlike ability to be surprised and delighted. It corrodes our channels of worship, and that disease is a terminal one.

It's not a new problem, of course. Jesus faced the cynics at every turn. Not only were the Pharisees incapable of partaking in the marvelous experience of His miracles and teaching, but even His own disciples constantly fell short of the grand concept. So many of His parables invited the hearers to wonder at the greatness of the kingdom of God, but nearly everyone missed the point. Finally, since they couldn't see the big picture, He gave them the small one. He held up a little child. The disciples were taken aback; they felt children weren't worthy of the rabbi's time, and they usually pushed them aside:

> But Jesus called them to Him and said, "Let the little children come to
> Me, and do not forbid them; for of such is the kingdom of God.
> Assuredly, I say to you, whoever does not receive the kingdom
> of God as a little child will by no means enter it."
>
> —LUKE 18:16–17

The primary theme there, of course, is humility. (Matthew 18 tells us that the disciples were arguing—*again*—about who would be the greatest in Jesus' kingdom.) But humility and wonder go hand in hand. Our faith needs to be childlike, not childish. We need to rediscover the *awe* of God. Much contemporary Christianity, we find, treats God in very casual terms as the ultimate Best Friend—which, of course, He is. But if we're not careful, we cut Him down to our size. Then our God is too small.

We don't need a convenient, compact god. We need the One who causes us to fall upon our knees, who leaves us speechless, who makes our eyes shine with His fire and causes us to depart as changed persons. And we need that God every moment of every day.

Recovering the Wonder

We'll close this chapter with five pathfinders for putting the wonder back into our worship. What do we need to know to approach God once again as little children?

- *We must be passionate about living every moment in the wonder of worship.* In this most worldly of worlds, we're swimming against the current if we want to live in God's presence. Do you really have an overmastering drive to know God intimately? Are you willing to spend each day in intimate relationship with Him? Those are the key questions for you today. The path begins with the passion.

- *We must know God rather than simply know about Him.* This point is obvious but essential. I hope you do become excited about the information in this book, but you can memorize every word and still have no experience of the presence of God—not unless you finally put the book down and approach the throne. Your mind is the beginning, but your journey to wonder leads through your heart. That's the part of you that God covets the most.

- ***We must serve God rather than simply identify with Him.*** Growth in faith comes through doing the things that Jesus would do. The Pharisees identified with God, and they had all the right information. But they'd lost touch with the needs of people. Serve someone today and tomorrow, and see if you don't encounter God in a more powerful way. Almost paradoxically, retreating into deep fellowship with God ultimately means having more experience with people. That's His agenda. Service will help you reestablish the wonder in your worship.

- ***We must worship God daily, which will require adjustments and sacrifices.*** As we'll see, sacrifice is at the heart of worship. Living every moment in the wonder of worship will change the way you live every day. It will require alterations in your thinking, your priorities, and your approaches to every portion of your life. Some of this will be painful. You'll be building a profile of obedience, and you'll be clearing away impediments that block the wonderful view. In the end, you'll count it all as loss for the perfect joy of knowing God.

- ***We will reap the rewards of living in the wonder of worship.*** As your life changes in this way, you'll feel a deep inner joy that you never thought possible. You'll be more devoted to God and better connected to family and friends. You'll be more focused and driven in your work. The crippling cynicism will melt away, and you'll be energized by the power of living faith. There are all these rewards and more.

But best of all, you'll become a child again, in every good sense of being a child. Every day will be Christmas morning, and every breath and opportunity will be bright gifts for your delight, all leading you to praise Him even more. And then, I believe, the light of your joy will begin to melt the despair and the cynicism of people whose paths you cross.

The glow in your eyes will outshine anything in the eyes of those reporters at the rocket launch in 1975. All they could see was a vessel bound for the heavens. You, however, will already dwell there—every moment of every day.

3

Where a King Makes His Home

THREE

 Where a King Makes His Home

THE CASTLE, IT WAS SAID, was among the most elegant in the world. Its turrets dominated the medieval sky, and the bright banners of the kingdom could be seen for miles. The throne room was embellished by gifts from many lands, and the walls were trimmed in pure gold. Everything sparkled and shone—everything but the gloomy face of the king.

The old monarch truly loved his people, from miners to merchants to mothers. He enjoyed their humble ways and ready humor, and he longed to hear the tales of their daily adventures, however humble and homespun they may have been. But few of the common folk were ever seen near the palace. For one thing, they were busy with their daily chores; for another, the gleaming citadel made them painfully aware of their lowly peasantry. Royal things made them uncomfortable.

So the good citizens looked only rarely to the gleaming towers, and they ignored the trumpets that heralded the comings and goings of the king. In time, they built their cottages and estates at increasing distances from the castle. They ignored the king's eager invitations to come and visit, even to enjoy his hospitality at the royal table. The people loved their king, but they preferred to do so from a distance.

The king grew lonely and despondent. He felt like a loving parent whose children venture into the world, never to return. He preferred to be more a guardian to be loved than a monarch to be feared. And so he came to realize that if the people wouldn't come to him, he must go to them.

The king instructed his courtiers to stay behind, and he walked alone to the town square. Naturally enough, the merchants and children recognized him immediately, and a hush fell over them. As they watched nervously, the king stooped down and began to play a game with two of the children. Soon there was a crowd of children all around him, and the men and women began to draw nearer too.

As the hours passed, the people found themselves coming to feel more comfortable with their king than ever before. In the past, he had been something like a distant rumor; now he was in the very midst of them, laughing and telling wonderful stories. They could touch his magnificent bejeweled crown. They see the twinkle in his eye. All the people marveled at his wisdom, and many shared their problems with him; he always had solutions. Most of all, a great love grew between them—a love for his kindness, a love for his kinship, a love for his kingliness. When the sun finally set, a lively crowd surrounded the king. Someone said, "Your Majesty, remain among us. We never wish to leave your presence, for we never knew how kind and joyful and wise you were."

And the king smiled as he replied, "You need never leave, for this is our kingdom together. From the most ancient of traditions, I must make my home yonder, in a palace of splendor. But I will leave you with a special gift." And with that, the king produced, from the crimson folds of his robe, a small flute. He placed it gently in the hands of a young girl. "When you return to your homes," he said to the crowd, "you will each find waiting for you a flute, a harp, or some musical instrument with your own name engraved upon it. Whenever any one of you plays the simple melody I will teach you, I will hear and I will come. This is the Praise Song of the King, and it will bring me to you wherever you may be. Even if only one of you longs for my company, that one has the privilege of playing my melody and calling my name. Your king's greatest desire, as I hope you will never forget, is your companionship."

And at that moment, the little girl's curiosity got the better of her. She gently puffed her breath into the flute, and the sound that emerged stopped all conversation. It was the most exquisite music any of them had ever heard, and it opened whole worlds of wonder to their astonished imaginations. As they soon understood, the king's very heart and soul were wrapped within that melody. It was as if great clouds drifted suddenly from their eyes, and the people could clearly see their king for the first time. All they had shared before was merely child's play—now, from the flute of a child, came something both joyful and serious. The melody told who their king was, and therefore it told them who they were.

When the king finally left, each citizen hurried home to discover his or her musical instrument. That village, as you might expect, was changed forever. In golden boxes the people kept and cherished their instruments. They played them every day, and somehow the king had time for each of them. They came to understand that he was really much more than a king. And as they played the ancient song, the instruments became more their own, more a part of them. The melody, they found, never became tiring or predictable, as other melodies do. It was ever deeper, ever more mysterious and wonderful, ever filled with new surprises.

Alone, one could play a beautiful song of the king in his or her own personal way. Together, the people could play their instruments and produce a symphony such as no human ear had ever heard. Either alone or together, they lived for the music, because somehow, through the world's deepest wonder, the king lived within the music. So the music lived on within them and filled their days.

Some say that the wonderful melody still drifts on the wind. Have you listened—can you hear it?

No Place Like Home

I expect you've already worked out the meaning of my little story. In every sense, God, our King, has come to us because we could not— would not—come to Him. He has done so through what we call the incarnation of Jesus, of course: dressing Himself in humble, human flesh to dwell among us in Jesus. But the implications go much deeper and are expressed in a startling concept that predates even Bethlehem. Wrap your mind thoroughly around this idea: *God makes His home in our worship.* The implications of that are so incredible that I tremble to write about them. God has given us an instrument for knowing Him, an instrument every bit as wonderful as that special flute. He has given us *worship.*

We should keep the following verse engraved in large letters in the fronts of our sanctuaries, on the covers of our church bulletins, at the center of our hearts: "But thou art holy, O thou that inhabitest the praises of Israel" (Psalms 22:3, KJV). Do you see the amazing proclamation of that verse? God makes His throne in the worship and praise that we offer in His name. The word we find in Hebrew, translated *inhabit* or *enthrone,* means "to sit down, to remain, to settle." One translation phrases it this way: "The praises of Israel are your throne" (NCV).

As someone once described this truth:

> Praise is where God lives. It is His permanent address. Praise is His home element. He is at home in praise. . . .
>
> This settles one of the vast mysteries which accompanies praise. Why is it that when we praise the Lord things change so rapidly? Why does healing come on wings of praise? Why do human emotions undergo such transition when praise is the choice? How are we to account for those things which accompany praise? The simple answer is: While God is everywhere, He is not everywhere manifested. He is at home in praise and, being at home, He manifests Himself best as God! . . .
>
> I spend much of my life in hotel and motel rooms across the world. I can get comfortable and enjoy almost any place. But I have a home to which I go often. It is there that you will find me in my natural element feeling "at home." . . . If you want to see God entirely "at home" and feeling comfortable, you may witness that happening in praise. God has an affinity for praise. He is enthroned and liberated to act mightily in praise.[1]

In his wonderful book *Reflections on the Psalms,* C. S. Lewis also writes about God's drawing near to His people through their praise and worship:

> When I first began to draw near to belief in God . . . I found a stumbling block in the demand so clamorously made by all religious people that we should "praise" God; still more in the suggestion that God Himself demanded it. . . . I did not see that it is in the process of being worshipped that God communicates His presence to men.

27

It is not of course the only way. But for many people at many times the "fair beauty of the Lord" is revealed chiefly or only while they worship Him together. Even in Judaism the essence of the sacrifice was not really that men gave bulls and goats to God, but that by their so doing God gave Himself to men.[2]

As you meet with God in the light of morning, as your thoughts turn to Him in the adrenaline rush of the day, as you move into the silent sanctuary on the Lord's Day—know that He takes His place upon the throne whenever you give Him your praise. Your bowed head, your humbled heart, and your attentive spirit open the door to heaven. It's a door that swings both ways, for we've already walked through it with John. But now God comes to us, no matter where we are. The wonder of worship is the wonder of His very real presence, and we feel something of what those villagers felt in the parable. It's music from another world, wonder that floods out all the darkness and the dust of death this life contains. We rediscover the innocence of children again as we praise and exalt God's name, for He opens Himself to us. It's the most awesome moment of life—more awesome than holding your first child in the delivery room, more awesome than meeting the person you're destined to marry, more awesome than seeing the earth from the window of the space shuttle. You've seen something more beautiful: the face of God Himself.

Try to create this picture in your mind. Imagine your Father relaxing into the cushions of His most comfortable easy chair with a sigh of satisfaction, luxuriating in the worship of His beloved child. That's what the Bible is telling us He does. *He inhabits the praises of his people.* He makes His home, His comfortable place of rest, in your heart and mine as we worship His name. When I'm away in lonely hotels, I can do what the citizens in that parable did. I can play the Praise Song of the King, and it brings Him to me. Or perhaps it takes me to Him.

This is all fine and good. But if worship is such a high priority—the one thing for which we have been created—how shall we then worship? What is that word all about, anyway? The word *worship* is almost like the word *love* in our society; it has been tossed around until it has been stripped of all meaning. It's a flute that has been coated by so much dust that it no longer seems to be capable of music; we're inclined to toss it on a dust heap. What a terrible mistake that would be! Instead, let's blow away the dust and take a fresh look at worship.

Let's find out what the Bible tells us about worship. Is sacrifice still necessary, such as they did in ancient times? What kind of music should we use? What are some good reasons for spending our time in worship? Is it really possible to worship God while we're at work or in a crowded shopping mall? What is meant by worshiping as an everyday lifestyle? How can worship help us in times of spiritual warfare? Each of these questions will be considered in this little book. Perhaps our discussion of worship will knock away a bit of that dust. Perhaps we'll put a shine on that old flute yet. But my greatest prayer is that you would summon your courage and place your lips to the flute. For if you do so, you'll hear the music. You'll feel the wonder. And you'll want to sing, "Joy to the world! The Lord is come!"

You'll be joyful because you'll feel His joy. And that will send the melody soaring even higher. You will be experiencing your very heart's desire—the wonder of worship.

4

A Temple on Wheels

FOUR

A Temple on Wheels

WE LOVE TO SPEAK of the way the Spirit of God comes to make His home within our hearts. That image has been a favorite one for Christian believers for a long time. Robert Boyd Munger's *My Heart—Christ's Home* is a beautiful example. This story pictures Jesus knocking on the door of a narrator's house and asking if He can come to reside there. He would like to be a closer friend and to make this house a personal home for Himself. The narrator agrees, and the rest of the little tale describes how Jesus walks through each of the rooms and makes various changes.[1]

The "rooms," of course, are merely symbols of the different segments of our lives. We give Jesus Lordship in the living room where family life plays out; we give Him control of the kitchen and the way we eat, of the recreation room where we decide how to spend our free time, and so on. There's a great deal of scriptural truth about devotion in that image of the human life as a home for God's Spirit. But it may be that there's a metaphor even more biblical and, believe it or not, even more compelling as to the way we live. I gave it some thought as I was exploring our topic of worship as an everyday lifestyle.

The analogy I'm thinking about can be found in Paul's two letters to the Corinthian church. As you may remember, this was a "Sabbath-only" kind of church. That is, people assembled for formal worship on the Sabbath, but none of the content of worship seeped over into their daily lives. All kinds of immoral and immature activities were going on among the Corinthians—thus Paul gave them a sizzling rebuke through the mail. I think that first letter must have burned their fingers when they pulled it from the mailbox. You'll recognize the sharpness in Paul's tone here:

> Or do you not know that your body is the temple of the Holy Spirit who is in you, whom you have from God, and you are not your own? For you were bought at a price; therefore glorify God in your body and in your spirit, which are God's.
>
> —I CORINTHIANS 6:19–20

Message: Stop holding out on God—He wants it all! Nominal Christianity is of no interest to Him. The Lord wants your body and spirit signed, sealed, and delivered over to their new Landlord. And as soon as He takes possession, that Landlord will convert the whole place to . . . another house? No, a *temple*.

That's what Paul says here. Would you engage in bickering and back-stabbing in a temple? Would you bring a prostitute there? (Actually, in the pagan religions from which many of these believers emerged, temple prostitution was a fact of life; Paul had his work cut out for him.) If God owns you, you've become a temple, so you'd better keep it tidy and sanitized. I bet the Corinthians had never thought of it that way. Paul returns to this striking word picture in 2 Corinthians, where he writes:

> And what agreement has the temple of God with idols?
> For you are the temple of the living God. As God has said:
> "I will dwell in them
> And walk among them.
> I will be their God,
> And they shall be My people."
>
> —2 CORINTHIANS 6:16

Jesus, you'll remember, compared His own body to the temple (see Matthew 26:61). As He lives on within us, we ourselves become the temple. If you want to see Paul develop the idea even further, you can find it in the latter part of Ephesians 2. In that striking passage, Paul describes how the unified body of believers, "being joined together, grows into a holy temple in the Lord" (Ephesians 2:21). We are *houses* for the holy, yes, but we're something even grander—we are *temples*.

But may I throw still a third item of architecture at you?

In 2 Corinthians 5, verses 1 and 4, Paul speaks of the body as an "earthly tent," a home not built to last. We may be ragged and torn, but we're destined for an eternal palace. Peter makes use of the same analogy (see 2 Peter 1:13–14). Paul, of course, knew more than a little on the subject of tents; he had constructed them for a living.

What is the significance of a tent? It's temporary and perishable, of course—but it's also designed for armies and people on the move. Keep that idea in mind as we move deeper into the concepts of temple and tent, and what they mean for our everyday lives.

ALWAYS SAYING "ALWAYS"

But for the time being, let's focus on temples. If we treat our bodies poorly in any way—whether through matters of diet, sexuality, exercise, or any other concern—we must realize we're desecrating the temple of God. He has bought us for the high price of the blood of Christ, and it's only fitting that we become structures worthy of the price. So we often quote this passage when urging our friends to care for themselves physically.

But I'm struck by the fact that Paul didn't say that our bodies were the mansion or the condominium or the vacation home of the Holy Spirit. The Spirit comes to reside within us as His daily residence, true. But Paul's analogy is a *temple*—a structure of holiness, a place of worship—and it's also a *tent,* a home for those constantly on the move. We think of that period in Israelite history when a tent *was* a temple. The laws of God, enshrined in the ark of the covenant, traveled with God's people and were guarded carefully in a special tent. In that way the people had a physical symbol for understanding that the holy presence of God traveled with them through all kinds of treacherous and foreboding landscapes.

The reason I belabor this analogy is that it suggests so many ideas about worship as a lifestyle. "Glorify God *in your body* and in your spirit," Paul writes (1 Corinthians 6:20b; emphasis added). *All* of life is worship. It's interesting to study Paul's use of one of his favorite words: *always.* Here are just a few examples (emphasis added):

- "Giving thanks *always* for all things to God the Father" (Ephesians 5:20a).
- "Praying *always* with all prayer and supplication in the Spirit" (Ephesians 6:18a).

- "Rejoice in the Lord *always*" (Philippians 4:4a).
- *"Always* laboring fervently for you in prayers" (Colossians 4:12b).
- "Rejoice *always,* pray without ceasing (1 Thessalonians 5:16–17).
- "May the Lord of peace Himself give you peace *always* in every way" (2 Thessalonians 3:16a).
- "Be steadfast, immovable, *always* abounding in the work of the Lord" (1 Corinthians 15:58a).

He also uses the phrase "without ceasing" on five occasions—in regard to praying for others, remembering others, thanking God, and praying in general. When we put all of these references together, his picture of the Christian life is one of unbroken prayer and communion with God. That includes (particularly when we look at what the *always* refers to most often) constant supplication for others, constant rejoicing, and constant thanksgiving. Paul particularly urges us to constantly thank God and constantly remember others in prayer. We could see these as the basis of the everyday worship lifestyle.

This is why I propose a new image of our lives before God—*a temple on wheels!* Why not? When we use Robert Boyd Munger's wonderful word picture, that of Jesus coming to the home, the idea is rather static and isolated. It involves Jesus visiting us privately, and we tend to think of divine fellowship as something that occurs at home. It's a nice, intimate picture—knowing Him personally.

But the Bible is giving us words like *always* and *without ceasing.* Are we to leave Jesus at home when we go out to the office or to the market? Obviously not. He goes with us everywhere, and we're constantly talking to Him; we're constantly rejoicing, thanking Him, and praying for those others whom we see along the journey. There's nothing static about *that* image—it's a relationship on wheels.

My Heart's Desire

Taking Your Act on the Road

Then there's another consideration that comes from the idea of your body as the Spirit's temple. We love Munger's analogy because it's comforting and warm: Jesus as best friend. But we're also concerned with worshiping Him as Almighty God, the Holy One, before whom all knees shall bow and every tongue confess His Lordship. There needs to be some awe in the equation.

That's the one element we lose in Munger's metaphor: the element of wonder, the dimension we've discussed that is so necessary in experiencing transcendent worship. This is why we dwell with God not simply in a home, but in a temple, just as Paul expressed to the Corinthians, who were living reverence-impaired lives. But we're not dealing with your ordinary, everyday temple. This temple is in the tattered tent of the human body. It's a temple that may look patched up and poorly sewn on the outside, one that will never last hundreds or thousands of years as those of stone may. But it contains the very presence of God just the same. It's better than a temple of stone, rooted to the ground. This is a temple in circulation.

There's a story from the dark days of the Second World War. So many things were in short supply then, and England needed silver for defense projects. Winston Churchill asked if there was any source of silver that had been left untapped. He was told that indeed there was— the churches and cathedrals had a few old statues of saints that had been cast in silver. Churchill smiled and said, "Well, it's time to put the saints back in circulation!"

That's the idea here. We, the saints, were never meant to be restricted to one roof. What if you began to see yourself as a saint in circulation, a temple on wheels, so that God could say, "I will dwell in [you] and walk [with you]. I will be [your] God, and [you] shall be My people" (2 Corinthians 6:16). What if you took your worship on the road, so that you rejoiced, prayed, expressed your thanksgiving, and exalted Him everywhere you went? You could think of yourself as a beautiful temple, a place fit for encasing the law of God, a place where all people could come to experience Him—for that's one essential element of a temple, isn't it? It's a place for others to come together in God's name. You may not have a ceiling and large rooms, but through you people can experience the living God just as they did in the old temple of Jerusalem. That's the very idea of having the Holy Spirit come to live within us. It isn't for the purpose of your having some private experience, but in order that we can serve God.

THE PROPER PICTURE

Perhaps you have some reservations about all this. Perhaps you have the mental picture of a religious fanatic, a "Jesus freak." You immediately envision one of those glassy-eyed, googly-grinned people who tries to corner you when you're out shopping and who lacks the capability to discuss anything but spirituality. You may be thinking, *If I acted like a temple at my office, and I walked around praising the name of God, rattling my Bible, and telling everyone I was going to pray for them—I'd last about five minutes!* Indeed, many of us feel intimidated about vibrantly expressing our faith today. And the workplace is more hostile to openly expressed faith. But let's take a moment to clarify our terms here.

First, please avoid using that mental picture of the religious fanatic. Who do you think puts those negative pictures in your mind when you attempt to envision committed Christianity? Here's a hint: He's the only one who trembles at the very thought of your living a passionate, worshipful life of service to the Lord. He wants to do anything possible to keep you from taking your faith seriously. So instead of thinking of an unattractive and unappealing "fanatic," think of a Christian leader you truly admire. Yes, it's possible to take Christ with you into the market-place or anywhere else *without* being offensively pious. That's the first condition.

Second, think about what God would be likely to do through you in relation to other people. For example, would He be eager for you to walk into a crowd and begin spouting religious rhetoric, thus antagonizing people and driving them away from Him? Or would He empower you to serve and counsel people at their point of need, and would He help you be a better and more attentive friend?

Third, rid yourself of those ideas that your life would become burdensome and joyless if you lived out your faith. I'm not certain how people come to think this, but it goes something like the following: "If I were to start ministering to people, and if I were to begin inviting them to my church, then I would lose some of my friends and I'd have no time for myself. My life is complicated enough!"

Let me ask you a question: How do you think God would feel if you became a temple on wheels? Do you think He would become more active or less so in your life? Do you think He would stop caring for you? Do you think you wouldn't feel tremendously blessed whenever you performed an act of ministry? Is your God big enough to help you live out your faith? Take your act on the road. Everywhere you go, God will be honored and glorified. There's nowhere you can go where He won't go with you, so there's no reason not to exalt Him in every place and in every endeavor.

But how? What would that kind of life look like? For the balance of this chapter, let's take a closer look at the dynamics of worship as an everyday lifestyle. We're going to discover four primary dimensions for putting your temple on the road.

Everyday Worship in Solitude

Worship as an everyday lifestyle begins in the simplest and most obvious terms. It's something every single one of us can do, yet something far too many of us overlook. If you want to live your entire life in the wonder of worship, you must begin with your personal time with God.

Perhaps you're disappointed that I would remind you of something so simple. Maybe you have a regular and committed quiet time already. But I believe it's impossible to be all that God intends for us if we're not willing to spend the time to get to know Him personally.

I also believe the best time for most people to get alone with God is early morning—it sets the tone for your entire day. God wants you to be the best and most effective servant possible, so He'll show you things and tell you things that will make the difference at crisis points during the next twelve hours or so. After you talk with the Lord and walk with Him through the schedule that lies ahead of you, He'll strengthen and encourage you to make every point of your day an act of worship.

Another advantage to a morning time with God is that He'll plant His Word in your heart. You'll be amazed at how often the very verse you studied over your morning coffee will have key significance a few hours later. Ask the Spirit to illuminate your study, and then go over your Scripture passage reflectively. Try to take that verse with you the rest of the day, so that it's never far from your mind. The Word of God is essential to the worship of God, and there's simply nothing so encouraging as His timeless and powerful Word. One little verse is enough to give you a divine perspective throughout the day. It will give you a sense of wonder to keep a worshipful frame of mind.

There are many other things that could be said about personal time with God, of course. And there are many good resources to help you along. The essentials, however, are two: you and the Lord, no one else, together and enjoying deep fellowship.

Everyday Worship in Service

How can we worship God while interacting with another person? Isn't that a contradiction in terms? Anything *but!*

One of the biblical terms for worship actually means "to serve." While the emphasis in the Old Testament had been upon worship that was law-based, the New Testament reveals a new kind of worship—one that is not law-based, but life-based. John 4 describes Jesus' penetrating encounter with the woman at the well. Her question was simple: Where is the proper place to worship—in Jerusalem only, or in the mountains? For the Samaritans, shunned and isolated, this was an important question.

Jesus told her that the time was coming when geography would no longer be an issue; God's people would worship Him "in spirit and in truth." Here we have it, the temple on wheels—a lifestyle enabling the spiritual element of worship to travel with us and become manifest in encounters such as this one between Jesus and a true seeker. This is the "new and living way" of worship (Hebrews 10:20) that makes it not merely private, but a social endeavor.

Listen to how Paul offers his mission statement: "That I might be a minister of Jesus Christ to the Gentiles, ministering the gospel of God, that the offering of the Gentiles might be acceptable, sanctified by the Holy Spirit" (Romans 15:16). He ministers to people because he sees them as a sanctified offering that God covets. And don't forget that in Romans 12:1, Paul urges us to offer our bodies as living sacrifices to God as our "reasonable service." Paul saw service as worship.

I could offer many other scriptural passages, but the point is clear. In serving others, we serve Christ, and we do so as acts of perfect worship. There may be a time when you help a stranger change a flat tire during a rainstorm, and you tell her, "I know this is what Jesus would want me to do." There may be another time when you make an anonymous financial donation to a good cause—no one knows but God, and it's an offering pure and fragrant in His eyes.

In service-based worship, you'll never forget that in every social encounter, even (or especially) with the least of these, you are glorifying the Lord. How might that mind-set change your social behavior, say, tomorrow?

EVERYDAY WORSHIP IN STRUGGLES

Another wonderful opportunity for everyday worship comes, perhaps, in the least likely of times—those occasions when we're confronted by a challenge. Stumbling blocks of daily life can become stepping stones to a divine encounter when we live with a Romans 8:28 mentality and worship God in the worst of circumstances. After all, that's the supreme test of our spiritual resolve, isn't it?

King Jehoshaphat faced such a moment when hostile armies were advancing upon Jerusalem. He prayed, "For we have no power against this great multitude that is coming against us; nor do we know what to do, but our eyes are upon You" (2 Chronicles 20:12b). He made a moment of anxiety into a moment of adoration, and the Spirit of God began to move in response. So many of the psalms were written in the midst of soul-wrenching agony, and they're supreme testaments of godly worship. Psalm 22 begins with Jesus' future gasp of anguish: "My God, My God, why have You forsaken Me?" It goes on to describe terrible pain, yet it comes to this conclusion: "All those who go down to the dust shall bow before Him, even he who cannot keep himself alive" (v. 29b). Even the one facing death bows in worship, for God has the final victory.

In *The Screwtape Letters,* C. S. Lewis wrote that when all is in turmoil and when everything has gone wrong and we feel spiritually dry, when we can't even feel God's presence, yet still we bow before Him, still we're obedient and prayerful—that's the time when God is the most pleased with us.[2] Despair turns quickly to victory when a broken heart is laid on the altar before God.

Yet we're not speaking only of those earthshaking trials. The little ones are actually the most elusive moments for the worshipful life. You're sitting in a snarl of traffic after a tiring day, and your nerves are frayed. What if you took that moment and reflected upon James 1:2–4? Sure, you *could* honk and gnash your teeth and bemoan your fate, saying, "I don't deserve this! Why should I sit in this gridlock?" Then again, you could also realize, "I'm counting this as joy! It means God is building something new and wonderful in my soul, and it will lead to me being perfect and complete, lacking in nothing—James says it and I believe it." Traffic suddenly looks entirely different as a new song comes into your heart. You take that splendid moment to turn your focus toward the praises of God as worship in everyday life.

EVERYDAY WORSHIP IN SACRIFICE

I wish to point to one final element of everyday worship. You can worship God through daily opportunities for sacrifice.

We have much to say elsewhere in this book about the true meaning of sacrifice. It's a concept that lies at the very heart of the idea of worship. Ultimately worship is expressed in a passage we've alluded to earlier:

I beseech you therefore, brethren, by the mercies of God, that you present your bodies a living sacrifice, holy, acceptable to God, which is your reasonable service. And do not be conformed to this world, but be transformed by the renewing of your mind, that you may prove what is that good and acceptable and perfect will of God.

—ROMANS 12:1–2

Paul is speaking, quite clearly, about everyday life. Most people are indeed conformed to this world. In the memorable paraphrase of this passage by J. B. Phillips, they "let the world squeeze [them] into its mold." But those who worship God in spirit and in truth, as heavy-duty temples on wheels, do just the opposite. They know the temple is a place for sacrifice. They transform everything and everyone, everywhere they go into an offering for God.

It's no easy matter to live that way. We're required to be obedient. We're required to submit to God and to sacrifice each moment, each relationship, each trial, and each setting to Him. It's a great deal easier simply to go to church and to submit an offering envelope with a bank check inside. But God wants a greater sacrifice than that. He wants it all. In the day and the week and the month that lies before you, you'll have countless opportunities for sacrifice. Think of that person at work whom you struggle to love. What if you visualize yourself placing that relationship upon the altar as an offering of praise to God? You have responsibilities you're not carrying out to the best of your ability. If you place them on the altar—right there within the moment of dealing with them—how will that change your performance?

Your marriage needs to be offered up as a sacrifice every single day. So does your parenting. So does the way you spend your free time. If you

45

began to make a list of the things you could offer up in sacrifice, you might never stop writing. The important thing is the idea *within the moment:* "Lord, I praise and exalt Your name, and I give this thing to You. Take my life and let it be consecrated, Lord, to Thee." The truth, you see, is that when your life becomes a temple, a home for Jesus, you begin to see His face in the faces of all those who surround you. You begin to treat them as you would treat Him. You begin to realize that all ground is holy ground, because God is there. You begin to see every situation as a potential act of worship, a time to magnify the name of the Lord.

Solitude. Service. Struggles. And ultimately, the one that encapsulates them all: sacrifice. Worship in the midst of these, and you'll become a temple on wheels. When that happens, be prepared to throw open the doors of your life. Believe me, you'll attract a crowd—the tent will become larger and larger. The world is waiting to see the person you will become when you live every moment in the wonder of worship.

5

The Wise Whys of Worship

FIVE

❦ *The Wise Whys of Worship* ❦

BRANTLEY HAS ALL THE SYMPTOMS. He seems to have come down with a case of common adolescence. There's a lot of that going around.

Brantley's bedroom door is closed much of the time and marked with a sign reading, "PRIVATE! Keep Out! THIS MEANS YOU! No trespassing! ABSOLUTELY NO soliciting, nagging, requests to turn down the stereo, do chores, or discuss my turbulent mood swings! Younger siblings may NOT use ANY of my stuff! Violators will be prosecuted!"

All attempts at conversation with Brantley are met with one of the following: (a) rolled eyes, (b) exasperated sigh, (c) the dreaded shrugging mumble, or (d) all of the above.

Mom and Dad are accepting all this with good humor—within reason. It hasn't been too many centuries, after all, since they navigated those same stormy waters, and they remember giving their own parents a rough voyage. They also realize that today it may be harder than ever just to be a teenager. Yes, Mom and Dad are trying to be patient, long-suffering, and available—again, within reason.

49

Just last night, a new domestic Brantley policy was announced. Henceforth, he let it be known, he would receive all his meals at the dinner table but take them to his bedroom for consumption.

"Nice try, but not so fast," said Dad. "We eat our meals together as a family, in one room at one table. It's been that way since you dined in a highchair."

Stony silence. Then Brantley said, "Well, I'm just doing this so you guys won't have to put up with all my rolled eyes, deep sighs, and the stuff you don't like."

"Thanks, but we'll survive the body language somehow. Dinner table attendance is an absolute, not an option, for this family."

"But why should I have to eat *your* way? What if I don't get anything out of sitting around the table hearing about your sales calls and Mom's PTA committee meetings and Kimberly's soccer team? I could be doing my homework or surfing the Net."

"The point is that some things are just right—such as families spending a certain amount of time together."

Dad has it right. The family dinner table is one of life's longstanding cross-cultural traditions for a reason: It's simply the right thing to do. We could list many other things that fall under that category. For instance, I know I must share my faith. I might do so with strangers on an airplane, or I might do so through inviting some neighborhood friends to a get-together. But Jesus has commanded me to spread the gospel, so I won't opt out.

Worship is another example. Like family life, it should be enjoyable. It should feed us and mature us, preparing us for life and leaving its stamp upon us forever. Worship and family life, when done right, are things we would never think to question. We would realize their value and beauty.

The Wise Whys of Worship

An Act of Obedience

Some people have come to believe that worship is an optional Christian activity. I've heard Christians say, "Bible study is the thing for me. I'm not much for singing hymns or mouthing praises. That's okay for people who go in for that sort of thing, but I'm more of a cerebral person, and I express my faith through studying."

Unfortunately that approach is never set forth in the Scriptures. Throughout the Bible we find that worship is no more an option than eating or breathing. Stop doing either of those and you'll die physically. Stop worshiping and you'll just as surely die spiritually. If you stop spending time together as a family, your family won't last. If you never share your faith, you'll never experience the greatest joy of serving God. And if you don't worship—and I mean *truly* worship, not simply attend a weekly service—you'll never experience God. It's that simple.

Imagine trying to make one weekly appointment to do all your breathing. Every Sunday you drive to the local oxygen tank, where you and a group of fellow air-breathers talk about the quality of the air, encourage each other to be better breathers, sing a few air songs, then do the week's breathing. Unfortunately, you'd be gasping for breath before you got back out of the parking lot. Worship in church is essential, but so is your personal, ongoing worship. You need to take it with you every day.

I recommend you take a few moments to breathe in the following verses from the Psalms. They'll nourish your spirit:

> Give unto the LORD the glory due to His name;
> Worship the LORD in the beauty of holiness.
>
> —PSALMS 29:2

Let us come before His presence with thanksgiving;
Let us shout joyfully to Him with psalms. . . .
Oh come, let us worship and bow down;
Let us kneel before the LORD our Maker.

—PSALMS 95:2, 6

For the LORD is great and greatly to be praised; . . .
Honor and majesty are before Him.
Strength and beauty are in His sanctuary. . . .
Oh, worship the LORD in the beauty of holiness!

—PSALMS 96:4, 6, 9

According to the Word of God, our Lord is to be loved by His creatures with all their hearts, souls, and minds. He is to be praised, blessed, gloried in, rejoiced in, exalted, feared, extolled, and thanked. We could add many more verbs. The idea is that we worship God with *all that we have*. Our worship comes from obedience and a grateful heart.

Worship isn't a spectator sport, but a *contact* sport. Each one of us is present to come into contact with the Spirit of God, and our worship happens not simply through hearing, but through being wholly involved in all that goes on as we come before God.

If you're going swimming, you don't stand forever beside the pool, dabbing a toe into the cool water. Ultimately the time comes to let go and dive in. There's no way to swim without using your whole body, unless you want to sink and drown. If you've ever tried to swim across a lake, you know that it takes a total commitment of your body, including your eyes, mouth, lungs, arms, and legs. That's why swimming offers some of the best physical exercise possible and why doctors heartily recommend it. It uses everything within you, all the muscles of your body.

Worship takes the same kind of spiritual commitment. Don't sit on the back pew, dabbing a toe into the deep spiritual waters. Dive into the wonder of the presence of God!

I believe many or most people worship for what they can get rather than for what they can give. But of course the paradox is that we take away the sum equivalent of what we've brought. I challenge you to try this the next time you worship, either privately or corporately. Ask God to show you how to give all of yourself to the acts of praise and worship. Tell Him you want to spring off the board into the deep waters of experiencing His awesome presence. Simply bring Him that obedient attitude and ask Him to teach you how to worship with all your heart, soul, mind, and strength. I guarantee you'll be more refreshed than the best swim you ever had!

AN ACT OF REVERENCE

The word *worship* comes from two words that really mean "worth" and "ship." The meaning of worship, then, is to give *worth* back to God, to assign Him His true and proper place. All of the trouble in the world comes from failing to do that. Every sin can ultimately be traced to failing to attribute the proper priority and Lordship to God.

Interestingly enough, some of the Hebrew and Greek words for *worship* are derivatives of the ancient practice of bowing to the ground as an outward sign of reverence. That's something we can do in both body and spirit. Worship, then, is the proper recognition and celebration of God, returning to Him the glory that He alone deserves and honoring Him with our lives and our words.

In Revelation 4:10–11 we find, perhaps, the ultimate image of worship. This scene occurs just before the one that began our journey—the scene in which no one is found who is worthy to unfasten the seven scrolls. There are twenty-four elders present, and they probably are representatives of Christ's church. These elders are clothed in white, and they're even wearing crowns. Yet they fall down in reverence and worship before the eternal King who sits upon His throne. They cast all that they are and all that they have before Him, and they sing:

> You are worthy, O Lord,
> To receive glory and honor and power;
> For You created all things,
> And by Your will they exist and were created.
>
> —REVELATION 4:11

This magnificent scene is a mental image to engrave into our hearts and minds, and it's nothing more than choosing to give back to God what He already deserves. In the days when John's Book of Revelation first appeared, the Romans were still at the height of their power. Any time a king was conquered by the Roman legions, he was either brought to Rome to prostrate himself before the emperor, or, failing that, he was required to bow and cast down his crown before a massive image of Caesar. The Romans demanded that any conquered king demonstrate his acknowledgment of the Roman emperor's superiority. The elders in John's vision wear crowns, but they show the same total submission to the King of kings and Lord of lords.

An Acknowledgement of Christ's Sacrifice

As we worship today, we sit on this side of the Cross. Compared to those who brought rams for sacrifice, we have a new relationship and a new experience in worship. We've been redeemed by the blood that was shed for us. We need no longer bring an animal—only ourselves. No priest or intermediary need be present for us to enter the holy of holies. We can worship in the very presence of God Himself, because Jesus tore away that curtain forever. That also means there's no longer a central location for all worship, as the temple once was. Your heart is where the action is now. Worship has become a "portable" thing—a temple on wheels, as we've called it.

When Jesus conversed with the Samaritan woman at the well, the two of them began discussing the proper place of worship. The woman recited the tired old controversy: Samaritans thought that any true worship must occur within the bounds of Samaria; the Jews thought that none of it counted unless it occurred in Jerusalem. Naturally she wanted to know Jesus' geographical coordinates for valid worship.

Jesus answered her very patiently. He told her the answer was "none of the above." At the time, people worshiped ignorantly. "But the hour is coming," He said, "and now is, when the true worshipers will worship the Father in spirit and truth; for the Father is seeking such to worship Him" (John 4:23).

The hour had arrived right there by the well—and the name of the hour was *Jesus,* for He had redefined worship forever. He was destined to die on the cross, and in the miracle of that moment everything would be made new. The veil in the temple would be torn forever, from top to bottom, a visual sign that the holy of holies was no longer a restricted club; it was open to all. At the foot of the cross, the ground was level for all who would kneel in its blood-spattered dust.

If we really understood all the depths of the implications of that fact, you and I would see worship in a brand-new way—we would see it as a celebration. It is an emblem of the greatest news that has ever been or ever could be. *Nothing* can separate us from the love of God. We think of worship in tones of dignity, somber faces, and dark sanctuaries. But isn't it true that worship is, in essence, the celebration of all celebrations?

When we become engaged for marriage, we throw a party. When we graduate from a fine institution after years of work, we invite all our friends to celebrate with us. When we're given the news that all our sins, those of yesterday and of today, are wiped clean once and for all; that the Spirit Himself has come to take residence in our hearts, never to leave us; that today we begin a transformation that will bring us every day to resemble Christ a bit more; that at any moment, in any setting, we can come boldly into the presence and the embrace of God Himself—are these realizations any less the occasion for joyful festivities? And yet we worship so often with downcast eyes, mumbled prayers, and absent thoughts.

My daughter Jan once said, "Dad, the only thing wrong with our worship is that we're running short on joy." I think she spoke wisely. This is not to say that worship should be undignified, but we can agree that it should always be drenched in joy, something that comes in many shapes and forms.

Here is what the great preacher Charles Spurgeon had to say on the subject: "When you speak of Heaven, let your face light up, let it be irradiated with a heavenly gleam, let your eyes shine with reflected glory. But when you speak of Hell—well, then your ordinary face will do."

Joy, it's been said, is the flag you fly from the castle of your heart when the King is in residence there. We need to raise those flags higher.

A REFLECTION OF YOUR LIFE

Professional football players have said that their performance on Sunday is a reflection of how they've practiced all week. Let me suggest to you that with worship it's precisely the opposite. We live during the week as a reflection of how we are worshiping—on Sunday or any other day. Worship is actually something like the State of the Union address for your life. It says how you feel about God at this moment in time, and it paves the way for how you will go on to live as a result. We approach God in a way that reflects the state of our present life.

In Romans 12:1, Paul writes, "I beseech you therefore, brethren, by the mercies of God, that you present your bodies a living sacrifice, holy, acceptable to God, which is your reasonable service." The New International Version translates that last phrase, "your spiritual worship." To come and lay ourselves upon God's altar—body, mind, soul, and spirit—we are saying, "Here I am, Lord! Make me Your instrument for heavenly music. Play it through me all the week long for your honor and glory. And let all that I do, all that I say, every place I go, every thought I think, and every relationship I have reflect my love for You and my worship before You."

During his brilliant career, the composer Franz Josef Haydn wrote the great oratorio *The Creation*. At the very end of his life, he was present to hear the music performed in all its magnificence. Haydn was old, worn out, and weak. They brought him in carefully in a wheelchair and attended to all his needs. The master composer was placed in a prominent place on one of the side stages where his failing ears might hear better. During the portion of the oratorio in which we hear God say, "Let there be light," the chorus and orchestra reach a crescendo. It's a musical expression of joy and praise, the magnificence of the creation. When this place was reached, there was an incredible reaction by all those present. Perhaps it was partially owing to the composer's presence. Perhaps it was simply that the performance itself was so majestic, so moving. The audience, overcome with emotion, rose as one to their feet and began cheering and clapping in joy.

All eyes turned toward the venerable old composer, who struggled to rise from his wheelchair. He centered himself on the side stage where everybody could see him, and he motioned for silence. An obedient hush fell across the great hall. With the limited strength in his arms, the composer pointed toward heaven and said, "No! No, not from me, but from hence comes all!" Then he quietly struggled back into his chair.

It was all to the glory of God—all the soaring music, all the ethereal harmony and transcendent joy. Every good gift is from above and points back to its source. Haydn knew that the rest is simply black notes on white paper. The greatest and most effective sermon I ever preach is to no glory but God's. The finest athletic performance by any Olympian is a tribute to the work of the Master's hand. The greatest work you will achieve this week—or through any peak performance of your life—is but a dim reflection of His *worth-ship*. At our best, we're not great canvases of art, but merely mirrors that reflect the divine light. We can never forget Haydn's lesson. Everything about our worship, whether in an easy chair with a cup of coffee and an open Bible or in the world's most beautiful sanctuary, must be a finger pointed to the sky, saying, "Don't look at me! Turn your eyes heavenward."

Could it be that if we drenched ourselves with that philosophy there would be less criticism of the church and of Christianity? Could it be that if we turned our faces toward the light of heaven, we would be molded to the image of Christ more swiftly and surely? Could it be that if we finally placed all that we have, all that we aspire, all that we are before God on the altar of worship, that He would return it to us filled with His light and transformed by His glory?

Let's not run short on joy. Let's stock up on it so that our homes, our churches, and our workplaces are overflowing with joy. Let's drench our everyday lives with joy and the wonder of worship. All we need to do is turn our eyes heavenward—and celebrate what we see.

6

All or Nothing at All

SIX

All or Nothing at All

S HE LIVED IN THE CITY OF LONDON, on the top floor of a tene-
ment building. She had brought her share of great dreams to the
great city. But what happened was beyond the wildest of them.

It happened, as always, without anyone expecting it. The building—
the place she called home—erupted in fire. Caught on the top floor, she
was trapped. As the fire raged out of control, a terrified young lady was
spotted in an open window, weeping and pleading for help. Every door,
every route of escape was cut off by the flames. To the heartsick crowd
that had gathered, it seemed she had only moments to live.

Suddenly, a ladder shot into the sky. It came to rest against her
window, and a courageous fireman took the young lady into his arms
and carried her downward to safety. Much like those unforgettable
American heroes at the World Trade Center, this public servant risked
his life to save another's life. Seconds later, the roof of the woman's flat
collapsed.

The scene, of course, was chaotic commotion. Neighbors were

61

laughing and crying, people rushed the exhausted young lady to a hospital, and in no time the fireman had seemingly vanished. She'd never even said thank you.

During the next few days, the young lady called the London Fire Department, talked to a few of the men, and discovered the name and address of her lifesaver. Over the phone, she finally and generously expressed her gratitude. The two young people began to chat, and an ongoing friendship developed from the conversation. Neither had a prior romantic attachment.

One fire had been snuffed out, but there were new sparks, this time of romance. Friendship grew into love, and love led to marriage. Much later, the young lady told her friends that she could never forget how her husband had saved her life. Without him, she knew she would surely have perished. But rescue and romance are two separate worlds. The fireman had become more than a lifesaver; he had become the object of adoration.

I think the problem most of us have with worship is that we've never made that "phone call"—the one where we seek to discover more about the One who has saved us. Many of us have a vague awareness that we've avoided hellfire, but we don't feel any particular emotional attachment to our Rescuer. Oh, we do give Him a call every now and then, whenever we need another rescue. "Help, Lord! I'm mired in financial problems!" Or, "Get the ladder again, Master! I'm out of work!" We see God as Someone who answers the 911 call, slides down the silver pole from heaven, and comes to rescue us from the flame—and politely disappears in the aftermath. We never take the step from salvation to adoration, from brief encounters to a deep relationship for every day and every moment.

If you and I can't imagine giving our lives in such a way, perhaps we

need to have a deeper experience with the Man on the wooden ladder—
the Man who stretched out His arms to show how much He loved us.

FIRST WORSHIP

All of this brings us to a man named Abraham. In this chapter and the
next, he will introduce us to an entirely new paradigm of worship—just
as he first introduced us to the Word itself.

Those who study the Bible in a serious way sometimes refer to the
Law of First Mention. It's not so much a law, really, as a common principle in the Scriptures. If you select an important biblical word—say,
worship—you'll find that its first biblical appearance sets the tone for all
the richness of meaning that will emerge. Through the Word we go on
to find many new understandings and many variations on the theme,
but the first cut is the deepest; the First Mention gives us the essential
picture.

So what of worship? We initially find the word in Genesis 18. Abraham
entertains three strangers who turn out to be the Lord and two angels. The
Scripture says that when he saw them, he "bowed himself to the ground"
(Genesis 18:2). The Hebrew word for his action is the one that we recognize as *worship,* and it's an essential understanding of the concept.

But the Scripture's first mention of the word *worship* as we understand it in a more formal sense—the intentional act of worship—is
found four chapters later. In Genesis 22:5, Abraham says, "Stay here
with the donkey; the lad and I will go yonder and worship." Abraham
has climbed the mountain with his son, whom he intends to offer in sacrifice. Most of us recognize this story with a twinge of pain—one of the
most gut-wrenching accounts in all the Scriptures. God has allowed
Abraham to wait for many years to have this child—not only his beloved

son, but the precious seed of a promised nation—and now the obedient father is asked to place the boy on the altar and give him back to God.

How have you responded to life's most frightening moments? Those are the times that identify what we're made of inside. At the very moment when Abraham's horrible time is at hand, Abraham gave it a curious name; one not found in the Bible before this occasion—not like this. He called it *worship.* He says, "The lad and I will . . . worship." Can you imagine a more profound, more moving portrait of the power of faith? Abraham is prepared to give all that he has, all that is precious to him, back to the One who gave it to him. It's the fireman rushing into the flames. It's the unreserved commitment to service through sacrifice. Abraham loved his son. Like any father, he would no doubt have given his own life to save this child. But God has asked him for something more demanding: to give Him the child. No more painful request could be imagined.

It's an all-or-nothing commitment—complete dedication. There's no way for us to be half-crucified with Christ. There's no way to pick up half the cross and follow Him. There's no way to be half-refined by the fires of purification.

True worship is true sacrifice. It's a hard truth, but it's only the beginning. Let's delve a little deeper into this profound ancient narrative.

Recognizing His Voice

We're told from the very beginning, in the first two verses of this narrative, that God was testing Abraham. An entire nation, God had told him, would proceed from him. The children of Abraham would outnumber the stars in the sky and the sands of the seashore. From his house all generations would be blessed (see Genesis 22:17–18). What kind of man was worthy to sire such a race? Abraham had to be tested in preparation, and he had to pass the most difficult test of all. You and I can see that clearly enough; how well Abraham could see it at the time, we may never know.

God calls Abraham and tells him exactly what to do. He tells him to go to the land of Moriah and wait for further instructions, at which time he will be giving his son as a burnt offering. It all begins, then, with his Master's voice. Worship comes as a command, not a suggestion. God tells Abraham where to make a sacrifice and what the sacrifice should be. Worship comes not as the fruit of our impulse, felt need, or creativity; it is the specific command of God. *Worship is God's idea.* It comes from the depths of His heart with the fullness of His passion. The very beginning of our journey into the depths of knowing God is marked by His voice calling us to come and worship.

It's worth pausing here to consider: What kind of story might we have without these first two verses giving God's command?

We'd have, to state it bluntly, a story of premeditated murder: infanticide, in fact, the ultimate horror. This would be far from a story of devotion and closer to a story of the demonic. It certainly couldn't be used, as it is in the Bible, to demonstrate the love and the plan of God.

But we do have the godly context. We have a God, in the introductory verses, calling His child to an act of burning, refining, purifying obedience that will test him to the deepest reaches of his heart. Then, in the concluding verses that make up our New Testament, we have the God who makes that same sacrifice, who puts His one and only begotten Son on the altar and offers Him in sacrifice—and this time the hand of execution is not restrained. So deep is God's love for us, so profound is His desire to bless all generations, that He Himself makes the sacrifice from which He finally stayed Abraham's hand. When we see the introduction and the conclusion, the beginning and the end, of God's command, we understand. And perhaps we, too, can only fall to our knees and worship in the midst of the ultimate pain and the ultimate love we see. This story becomes not a curious enigma, but holy ground, in which we experience God in a deep way.

Abraham recognized His Master's voice, and so do we.

Responding to His Command

Genesis 22:3 tells us that Abraham "rose early in the morning." He made all the preparations for his journey, saddling his donkey and summoning two servants. Then he awoke his son, Isaac. He must have felt he was looking upon the peaceful slumber of his boy for the last time. Abraham split the wood for the fire and then set off for the destination God had named. Think of how melancholy all these tasks must have been. Each gave him an opportunity to reconsider and to rebel. Perhaps he had imagined that voice from heaven. Perhaps he could procrastinate and wait for better weather or for God to change His mind. Perhaps Abraham could pretend he'd never heard the command.

Put yourself in Abraham's sandals. What if the voice of God came to you today with such a request? What would you do?

I can well imagine it, for I have children of my own. If God ever called upon me with such a command, it would take me two minutes to be on the phone to my circle of pastor friends. I'd ask them to help me interpret what I had heard from God. Every statement I made, every nuanced phrase, would be bent on getting my friends to convince me I had heard wrong. I would ask my advisers to help me somehow come to that conclusion. Then I would take some time off to pray and reflect—as much time off as it might take me to comfortably rationalize the simple command of God.

At least I suspect that I might do something of the kind in the face of such a difficult command, and you might do the same. A dying W. C. Fields, according to legend, surprised a friend by asking for a Bible. When he asked the comedian what he was doing, Fields replied, "Looking for loopholes." And we all do a bit of that when it comes time for truly sacrificial obedience.

But not so with Abraham. The Bible details his every action, each of which was one more step down the thorny path God had laid out. As a matter of fact, we're told that Abraham rose early in the morning to get a head start on the most difficult assignment he'd ever faced. He didn't call in sick. He didn't look for loopholes. Abraham set out for what the Lord had defined for him as worship, and he did so without question.

Robert E. Webber has written a helpful book entitled *Worship Is a Verb*. When I came across that striking title in a bookstore, I was intrigued. Webber's thesis is that worship isn't a feeling or a thought process. It's something much greater than a mere emotion. Worship, he says, is an activity we pursue in obedience to God's directive. It is far from passive, but something in which we participate wholeheartedly, something we can do every moment of every day.[1]

Let's not gloss over that point; it's not as self-evident as it may at first appear.

For too many of us, worship has become as participatory as an NFL football game. Perhaps we watch on television; perhaps we venture to the stadium to sit in the stands. But the only experience we have of professional football is the *vicarious* kind. Similarly, many people sit in pews or watch televised preaching—but that's spectator sport, not worship. It's casual and detached. God calls us forward from the sofa, the pew, and the aloofness by which we keep a safe distance. He calls us, as He did Thomas the doubter, to step forward and feel the wounds in His hands. He calls us to confront the mystery of His manifestation. He calls us to take a central and dynamic role in the adventure, the lifelong quest, of knowing Him. It only happens when we take our worship not as a noun, but as a verb and get busy doing it.

God called Abraham to step forward. And no matter how reluctant he might have felt, Abraham obeyed. He obeyed by rising early, by saddling the donkey, by summoning the servants, by splitting the wood, and by walking the road. The experience of the heart begins with the work of the hands. We must respond to God's command with the initiative of physical action.

RETURNING OUR BEST

The second verse of our passage is a difficult one for me to read. It never fails to bring a lump to my throat and a tear to my eye. God says to Abraham, "Take now your son, your only son Isaac, whom you love, and go to the land of Moriah, and offer him there as a burnt offering" (Genesis 22:2).

As we've seen, Abraham's boy was everything to him. We all love our children, and every single one is special and unique. But this one was *especially* special; this one had been waited for, prayed for, hoped for, and finally rejoiced over when he arrived after many decades of anticipation. Only to be burnt like an animal? The mind's obedience and reason aren't always in perfect harmony.

This is a passage we struggle to comprehend as we read it in Genesis. Not until Hebrews, clear on the other side of our Bibles, do we finally see all the puzzle pieces in place. I'll never forget the first time I read this verse carefully. My jaw almost hit the floor! Hebrews sheds quite a light on Abraham's test:

By faith Abraham, when he was tested, offered up Isaac, and he who had received the promises offered up his only begotten son, of whom it was said, "In Isaac your seed shall be called," accounting that God was able to raise him up, even from the dead.

—HEBREWS 11:17–19

It's quite simple: Abraham had received a promise. He had the assurance of God that Isaac would be part of a great line of people who would bless the world. But now God was asking for the child to be given in sacrifice. God doesn't break His promises, so the only conclusion left open to Abraham was that the Lord would have to raise Isaac from the dead! Such was the trusting spirit of Abraham, willing to literally put his faith under the knife.

Abraham had to come to that altar completely as he was, questions and all. "Here am I, Lord," he must have said. "I don't understand. I'm not without deep fear and misgivings. But obedience is my true sacrifice. It's obedience that I lay on this stone before you. Obedience and trust. You will never fail in Your promise, and I must never fail in my obedience."

Abraham laid all these things on that altar. He laid down his questions, his confusion, and his emotions. He laid down his faith and his obedience. It was all a test of priorities, to reveal what finally stood, what Abraham would cling to when all else was stripped violently away. How would you pass such a test? Would you worship in complete obedience if all else in the world were removed—if your every worldly possession, every beloved relationship, every fond hope and dream were lost to you? What would God ask you to place on the altar of testing in your life?

It's quite a question for you and for me, but perhaps it's the central question of worship. I don't know where your primary place of worship is, whether in your quiet study or the church pew. It's probably a very comfortable place. But what if it weren't quite so comfortable? What if worship demanded of you the thing that you valued most in the world? In that moment you would find out a great deal about yourself. You would hear the voice of Jesus whispering over your shoulder that "where your treasure is, there your heart will be also" (Matthew 6:21). Unless you had a tough, spiritually disciplined mind, conditioned by a life of ongoing and everyday worship, you might well be overcome by the challenge.

In this moment of clarity and refinement, Abraham demonstrated what was inside him, and how deep it went. You could go down to the very depths of his soul, beneath all the loves and values and priorities that moved him, and his faith sank deeper still. It stood firm.

How does the Lord respond to that depth of worship?

> By Myself I have sworn, says the LORD, because you have done this thing, and have not withheld your son, your only son—in blessing I will bless you, and in multiplying I will multiply your descendants as the stars of the heaven and as the sand which is on the seashore; and your descendants shall possess the gate of their enemies. In your seed all the nations of the earth shall be blessed, because you have obeyed My voice.
>
> —GENESIS 22:16–18

Oh, how God longs for us to be pure-hearted in our obedience. The floodgates of heaven would open with His joy and blessing. But are we committed—*totally* committed?

Perhaps you've heard that story about the little boy whose younger brother was gravely ill. A blood transfusion was needed, and a sibling is often the best match for such a transfer. The parents took the little boy aside and gently explained the need to him. "Your blood might save your little brother's life," they said. "Without it, he could die."

The little boy sadly nodded and agreed on the transfusion. As the nurses were preparing the instruments, they asked him to close his eyes and relax. He asked, "Will it happen quickly or slowly?" They told him it wouldn't take long to collect the blood. "But how long for me?" he asked, still not satisfied. It turned out that the little boy had not understood; he thought he was giving not only his blood, but his life. He was willing to do so to save his little brother.

That's all-or-nothing commitment. It's pursuing the object of adoration right into the flames. The Lord longs to bless us when we worship Him truly; Abraham found that out. It was a moment of surpassing holiness, and I believe that particular mountaintop became, at that moment, holy ground. In the next chapter, I'll show you why—and the answer may surprise you!

7

This Hallowed Ground

SEVEN

This Hallowed Ground

O
N AN EVIL DAY, the ark of the covenant fell into enemy hands. The enemies of God's people captured it and stowed it among the other plundered treasures of their defeated foes.

Imagine the demoralization of the Israelites. This beautiful golden casket was the receptacle that enclosed and protected the tablets of the law of God—the holy tablets carved by the finger of God and brought down the mountain by Moses. The ark was the great symbol of God's presence and guidance. It had been among God's people when they crossed the Jordan. It was there when God toppled the walls of Jericho. Through the peaks and valleys of the time of the judges, the ark had been a present and powerful reminder that God was with His people, that His laws were sacred. But the Philistines seized the ark on the battlefield at Ebenezer.

What happens when pagans take hold of something that sacred, that essential? Remember, the Israelites didn't possess the ability to worship without the benefit of the high priest and the trappings of the temple—

not like you and I have. The ark was no mere symbol. It was their precious link to God Himself.

There was misery for the Israelites, but the Philistines fared no better. They thought better of their prize when the strange, captured crate brought them seven months of plagues. Thus the ark came right back, a treasure no longer desired. David took it on parade through the streets of Jerusalem. There was shouting and laughter as the procession made that last lap. There was dancing and rejoicing, celebration and worship. David placed it in a tent, and the ark was home again.

But as David reflected on the amazing journey of the tablet, his joy began to fade. Something wasn't quite right. "See now," he said, "I dwell in a house of cedar, but the ark of God dwells inside tent curtains" (2 Samuel 7:2b). God deserved only the very best; He deserved the finest temple human hands could possibly fashion. It would fall to Solomon, David's son, to carry out the great construction—this was a matter of God's timing—but it was David who was first stirred with the passion to give God the very best as a place of worship.

David began to scout out locations for the great temple he was visualizing. The Scripture says he found a place he liked, the threshing floor of Ornan the Jebusite. David went to Ornan and told him what was in his heart. He described the greatest place of worship imaginable, a place where people would come into God's presence for time immemorial.

David told Ornan he was prepared to buy the property. But after listening carefully, Ornan replied that he could never accept payment for land that would become holy ground; no, the property must be his gift of love.

Most of us would have smiled at that point and praised Ornan's generous gesture. But not David, for he understood a profound principle you and I tend to miss. He shook his head and said, "No, but I will surely buy it from you for a price; nor will I offer burnt offerings to the LORD my God with that which costs me nothing" (2 Samuel 24:24).

Some things in life must carry a cost; they can't come free or cheap. Worship is one of those. Many of our worship events have become so relaxed, so frivolous and informal that not only do they cost us nothing, but they are more focused on entertainment than sacrifice. David's insistence on a financial transaction may have been the simple gesture of a wealthy man, but it was grounded in the sober realization that worship must be built on a foundation of sacrifice, of bringing to the altar the best, and *only* the best, that we have. It shouldn't come free, and it shouldn't pass lightly.

LEGACY OF THE LAND

Now are you ready for the surprise? When the temple was finally built by David's son, it rested on the very ground where Abraham once laid his beloved son on the altar.

In the preceding chapter, we began our exploration of that profound event; in this chapter we'll complete the journey. And already we see that in the Bible's equation, true worship for the people of God begins, then reaches its fullest expression, on the site where the validity of Abraham's worship was put to the test. By extension, many more holy events are tied to that little plot of land, a focal point of history to this very day.

The fate of Jesus, for example, was played out on that spot. So many events of the crucifixion week came to pass on the very ground where Abraham, David, and Solomon had their great moments of revelation. Jesus went so far as to identify Himself with the temple, saying it would be destroyed and rebuilt in three days. Predictably enough, that statement caused a great deal of commotion and led to the charges that brought His arrest. But Jesus' double meaning was that His body would be destroyed and then raised. In A.D. 70, the temple itself would be destroyed.

The double meaning was intentional, because Jesus became our temple—the receptacle of God's law and presence. Today, a tour of Israel will bring you to a spot called The Dome of the Rock, which is the very place we've been discussing. At this point in time, the Muslims, who have decided that Muhammad and his horse ascended to heaven from here, have control of this site. But the final page has yet to be written. We're told this very plot of land in ancient Jerusalem, the place where Abraham went with his son by his side and a tear in his eye, the place where David stood and visualized the greatest temple to be built by human hands, the place where Jesus taught the elders as a boy and then confronted the Pharisees as a man—at this same site, another temple will someday rise in glory and magnificence. The holy ground of Abraham and Isaac, where an angel stopped an old man's hand so long ago, has yet to see its destiny be fulfilled.

Make no mistake—Abraham's test is more than a touching Bible story. The deepest mysteries of humanity and our relationship with God are bound up there. The greatest mystery of all is that true worship is truly costly. During the past few years, I've learned this truth more and more deeply. I no longer want to give God the superficial and the frivolous. I no longer want to hold back from Him the best and the dearest things. I don't want to *play at* worship any longer, but to worship God in spirit and in truth. I want Him to have the very best of my attention, the very deepest of my sacrifice, the most profound of my music and teaching and feeling as I enter into His presence.

I want those I care for to approach God in the same way, and I will watch to see if it is happening. My prayer is to see a community of worship all around me—people experiencing the manifest presence of God as they go to their offices, clean their homes, care for their children, arrive at our church, and go home again. I'd like to see them already praising the Lord when they get here and continuing to do so as they leave. That's a lot to ask for, but what it costs is irrelevant. What it accomplishes is everything the heart could wish.

RETREATING TO HIS SOLITUDE

I noticed something else interesting about Abraham's preparations to go to Mount Moriah. The fifth verse of Genesis 22 tells us that Abraham left the young men behind. He told them to stay with the donkey and wait as he took Isaac on the last leg of the journey. All this way he had come—why would he make a point of leaving his servants?

He did so because worship is personal. It's one-on-one with God. Yes, we worship together as the body of Christ. We're commanded to do so, and yet even in that context we must worship from the depths of our individual souls. Abraham traveled light for the worship portion of his task, taking only Isaac and the wood he would need for the fire.

Have you found that to be a great challenge in your personal worship? You come to the place of worship carrying many burdens, and when you come to the door of the holy of holies, you find room enough only for *you* to fit through—no backpacks, no suitcases, no packages. Everything else must be set down and left behind you. When you emerge again, glowing from an encounter with your Lord, you'll no longer see the need to carry that cumbersome baggage.

Yet it's so difficult to lay down your burdens at the point of worship. You're straining to keep your mind on that psalm you're reading, your thoughts on the hymn. You're pouring out your heart in prayer, yet your mind keeps wandering to the emptiness of your stomach or the cares of the day. Our minds are held captive by anxieties that are as nothing in the floodlight of His beauty and power. In fact, the very best way to deal with any of them is simply to give them to God. And yet again, we struggle to lay down our burdens. We find that we cannot fit through the door to worship, the door that is precisely the size and shape of our unfettered souls.

Our concerns will follow us even as Abraham's faithful young men did, but those concerns belong to our Master. We must at some point turn to them, as Abraham did, and say, "Stay behind me."

We who are church leaders have been the worst offenders. At one time I realized our church was beginning our services well, starting to bring our people into the transforming presence of God—then would come the time in the service when we'd send out the "Minister of Announcements." We would have him spend ten minutes giving our people more details to remember, more events to plan, more burdens to hold them back from the immediate, present event of worship. As a matter of fact, we did everything we could to make those announcements exciting and enticing. We would use humor, build excitement, and captivate imaginations. That was good promotion of activities but poor stimulation of worship. I realized that the purpose of the service was to bring our sheep before the Shepherd. We were dragging our people out of the holy of holies and dropping them onto the pavement of the temple courts, where there was always commotion and chaos. We have tried everything from using slides to announce our activities to postponing all announcements to the end of the service. We still struggle!

On a personal basis, this is the very reason Jesus tells you to go into your closet rather than to pray in public. We're told in the Scriptures that He Himself left early in the morning and sought solitude so He could be with His Father.

Worship is personal business, and you must make the final approach alone. Distractions must be eliminated./Circus-like announcements inserted into the middle of worship are like reading your mail in the middle of your personal devotions./We need to make a discipline of *retreating* in body, mind, soul, and spirit. Some of this will be physical retreat for you, of course—and you need it every day. But you'll also need to cultivate the discipline of taking your thoughts captive for God's Spirit as you go about your daily business. Give the Lord an ever-present corner of your mind and Spirit, so that His influence will guide you even as you do the most mundane activities. That's the personal business of everyday worship. We need to do it better as individuals and as bodies of believers.

REJOICING HIS HEART

Imagine, if you will, that you're one of the servants Abraham left behind. How do you think the old man looked as he took his son arm in arm, apparently for the last time, got a good grip on the kindling, and trudged up the mountain? Abraham was obedient, but that doesn't mean he was dispassionate. His face must have told a story of profound grief. He was a hundred years old but looked much older on this day, if that could be possible. The servants must have wept in terrible commiseration as they watched his bent and burdened figure disappear at the crest of the rise.

Imagine now the sequel. You and the other servants are sitting around a campfire, talking quietly, speculating on future life with your mourning master. And here comes Abraham, not slouching, but nearly bounding into the circle of campfire light! How could this be?

Then you see the figure behind him, Isaac—still alive and well. But there's no guilt, no furtive look of disobedience in the face of Abraham. There is only deep joy, laughter dancing in his eyes, light radiating from his demeanor. It seems as if years have been drained away from his life. He's had a joy transplant. Soon he has told you the whole story, and everyone is spontaneously worshiping God with the master. It's hard to decide which outweighs the other: laughter or tears.

And who is happier: Abraham, who has been relieved of the dreadful task, or Isaac, who has received a stay of execution? For we cannot forget that this son humbled himself and was obedient to death even as another Son would do, near this very spot, many centuries later. Isaac had asked, "Father, where's the sacrifice?" And his father had replied that God would provide it. When the father had raised the knife, Isaac could have fled. He was not a child, but a young man of health and vigor. Abraham had been required to trust the goodness of a perfect God, but Isaac had been required to trust the faith of his human father. And he, too, passed a great test that day.

You'll remember the ram that was caught in the thicket. This was, to Abraham's delight, the true sacrifice "God would supply," and soon the more conventional ritual was carried out. Abraham was filled with joy, but don't forget that in his heart he had already killed his son—he'd had to do that the moment he determined to be obedient. In his mind and heart, he'd had to give him up; that was the test. Abraham's son had been dead to him for a terrible period of time between God's command and the angel's staying his hand. And now both God and Abraham knew something.

God knew that Abraham had absolutely no other gods before Him. He knew that Abraham's heart and devotion to Him were pure.

And Abraham knew the same thing about God, who had loved Him not only in preventing the loss of Isaac, but also in the wonderful blessings that God had spoken to Him in the aftermath of Abraham's obedience. True worship pleases God, and when that happens, He blesses us in the deepest and most gratifying ways the soul can experience. The blessing upon Abraham bears rereading:

> By Myself I have sworn, says the LORD, because you have done this thing, and have not withheld your son, your only son—in blessing I will bless you, and in multiplying I will multiply your descendants as the stars of the heaven and as the sand which is on the seashore; and your descendants shall possess the gate of their enemies. In your seed all the nations of the earth shall be blessed, because you have obeyed My voice.
>
> —GENESIS 22:16–18

Such is the joy of God when we simply give Him what has been His all along—the devotion and worship He merits. We give it because it is right to give it, and not out of some selfish motive. But we can't help observing the truth that we reap what we've sown. True worship from the soul puts a smile on God's lips, and life is good when God finds us faithful. No matter what you may bring to your Lord, no matter how deeply you may sacrifice, you'll never give more deeply than the return He will bring, simply because He delights in you when you delight in Him. He will bless you, but He will also bless the world through you.

Worship unlocks the gates of heaven and floods your world with light.

WORSHIP IN THE RIGHT KEY

In the late nineteenth century there lived a young man who became the prototype of the sports superstar. His name was C. T. Studd, and he was the greatest cricket player in England. He may have been the first athlete whose name became a household word. While he was studying and playing cricket at Cambridge, Studd gave his life to Christ after hearing D. L. Moody preach a revival. C. T. Studd made a wholesale, absolute dedication of his life to the cause of Christ—wherever he might be led and whatever the cost might be. He and the "Cambridge Seven" were like today's Athletes in Action movement; they traveled everywhere using their sporting fame to speak for Christ and winning impressive numbers of converts.

Studd went to China and later to India as a missionary. It was in China that word reached him that he had inherited a substantial financial fortune. Immediately, he donated all of it to the works of Jesus Christ. Studd could have lived a life of comfort and wealth, trading off his youthful fame. But he didn't see that as his deepest worship.

Just before Studd left for China, he spoke at a great meeting. There was a young preacher in the crowd named F. B. Meyer, already well on his way to becoming one of the great Christian scholars and ministers of the day. Meyer was profoundly moved by the testimony he heard that evening. It wasn't the words, he explained, but the demeanor—here, in C. T. Studd, he saw for the first time in his life a man utterly and unreservedly committed to Christ. After the meeting he sought out the athlete and said, "Young man, you have something I lack and something I need. That's more than obvious. But I can't put my finger on what that thing might be. Could you tell me?"

C. T. Studd knew he was speaking to a great man, a very prominent figure in Christian circles. But he didn't hesitate in his reply. He said, "Have you surrendered everything to Jesus Christ?"

F. B. Myer thought a moment and said that, yes, he felt reasonably certain he'd done that. Then he turned and left, even as the little voice in the back of his mind kept rebuking him, telling him he hadn't answered the question with integrity. When he arrived home, he went straight to his bedroom and fell on his knees. The prayers and the deep emotions flooded forth from his soul. But he listened, too, to see what God might say. And it seemed to Meyer that the Lord walked right into the room and spoke to him. The Lord had held out His hand and said, "Meyer, I need them all—I need the keys to your heart." Meyer began to have it out with God. But the empty hand still confronted him. Finally, in his vision, Meyer reached into his pocket, withdrew a great ring of keys, and handed them over. He waited while they were counted, one by one, but the Lord looked up finally and said, "There's one missing. I asked you for all of them."

And He turned and walked out the door.

Meyer called after him, "Wait, Lord! Where are you going? Please don't leave me!"

The Lord smiled sadly upon him and replied, "If I'm not Lord *of* all, Meyer, I'm not Lord *at* all."

"But, Lord, it's just a small key, just one among a great ring of them, just *one.*"

"If I'm not Lord *of* all," repeated the Lord, "I'm not Lord *at* all."

With great, desperate weeping, F. B. Meyer agreed to turn over that last tiny key. He surrendered everything he was, everything he had, and everything he might ever be, to his Lord. And from that day on, the Lord began to use Meyer as He never had before—as He has used few people, to state it frankly. The Holy Spirit came and brought incredible power to that ministry, and the sermons and books of F. B. Meyer are still bearing fruit to this very day, a century and a half later. Like Abraham, Meyer saw generations yet unborn blessed by the goodness of God because of his act of complete, painfully sacrificial worship.[1]

The final shining key of worship is the statement from your lips that says, "Lord, there is nothing in my life that I love more than You. There is nothing I will hold back. There is no person or thing I'm not willing to leave behind. I surrender all." He already has the key to your church involvement; He wants the "skeleton key" that opens every single door to any compartment of your life. I can't tell you the greatness of the splendor of His opening all those dark doors and letting in His light and glory. All I can do for you is express my joy and take your hand, as the apostle Andrew did for his brother, and say, "Come and see!"

8

The Language of Angels

EIGHT

The Language of Angels

IN THE BEGINNING, when darkness was upon the face of the deep, a billion bright eyes pierced the blackness of space, and they began to pour out a cosmic symphony. We have Job's assurance of this event: "When the morning stars sang together, and all the sons of God shouted for joy" (Job 38:7).

Can you imagine anything so magnificent? How could the majestic act of creation be accompanied by anything other than the music of the spheres? Angels and starlight sang their hallelujahs as God's fingers wrought the masterpiece of the universe. And from the time He gave us life and breath, we've looked to the heavens and found ourselves unable to refrain from singing.

Melody takes up where mere words leave off. It fills in the blanks of our wonder and praise. It is the stamp of eternity set in the deepest reaches of the soul. How could we worship without it? How could we endure life without it? When the cities of Afghanistan were liberated from the radical oppression of the Taliban, the first thing the people did was to play their music, which had been forbidden. Nothing is more humanizing than melody—yet nothing points more surely to heaven.

For those of a bent "too serious" for such frivolities as music, the fact remains that there are 575 references to praise, singing, and music in the Bible. At the very center of the volume is a 150-song hymnal known as the Psalms. From the beginning, music has been an essential link between God and His children. In fact, there are more verses about praise than about prayer. God set all His creation singing—"and heaven and nature sing"—from the melodies of the birds to the song of the whales. Animals, it is true, use music in a utilitarian fashion. But it is only men and women, created in the image of God, who can make intelligent use of pitch, tone, and harmony to focus their praise and express their heartfelt emotions.

How did Mary respond when the angel visited? She sang. How did the early Christians express their faith when gathered together? They sang. How did Paul and Silas occupy themselves when the Romans took them prisoner? "Singing hymns to God" (Acts 16:25). By the way, we never hear about Pharisees having a sing-along. And what is the activity that we're all so certain will occupy us in eternity? Singing praises to God. Heaven is the birthplace of music. It's been observed that you can't imagine hell with music nor heaven without it.

John, through his apocalyptic vision, gave us a beautiful picture of what we might call the "song of the throng" that awaits us in heaven:

> After these things I looked, and behold, a great multitude which no one could number, of all nations, tribes, peoples, and tongues, standing before the throne and before the Lamb, clothed with white robes, with palm branches in their hands, and crying out with a loud voice, saying, "Salvation belongs to our God who sits

on the throne, and to the Lamb!" All the angels stood around the throne and the elders and the four living creatures, and fell on their faces before the throne and worshiped God, saying:

"Amen! Blessing and glory and wisdom,

Thanksgiving and honor and power and might,

Be to our God forever and ever.

Amen."

—REVELATION 7:9–12

Another John, one with the surname of Newton, captured it in the last verse of his song "Amazing Grace":

When we've been there ten thousand years,

Bright shining as the sun,

We've no less days to sing God's praise

Than when we'd first begun.

Eternity is that place where time falls away, and we'll fill infinity itself with the music of God's praise. Think of this: The highest expression of praise our minds can fathom is the expression of singing. Perhaps it's time to think a little more deeply about matters of music.

MIND AND MUSIC

There are a number of wonderful attributes of music. One of them is that music increases the effectiveness of memory. How much easier is it for us to remember passages of the Word of God because someone set them to music?

From our earliest years, if we were fortunate, the essential truths of

91

our faith were implanted permanently in our hearts through Sunday school choruses such as "Jesus Loves Me," "Jesus Loves the Little Children," and "This Is My Father's World." Those simple songs contain no less than the keys to the greatest problems of our world. What if the whole world stopped to sing, and to believe, these words:

> Jesus loves the little children,
> All the children of the world,
> Red and yellow, black and white,
> They are precious in His sight,
> Jesus loves the little children of the world.

This gift can be used for ill, of course. F. Olin Stockwell was one of the last missionaries out of the People's Republic of China. He tells, in *Meditations from a Prison Cell,* how the Chinese indoctrinated their young people. By the hundreds, their youth spent their mornings in study. But in the afternoons, they would sit in the presence of a leader with a pitch pipe, who used simple songs to teach phrase after phrase of the communist dictum. The young people learned all the doctrines of hate and fear and domination by way of melody.[1]

Music teaches and trains, and it does so with a power that speaks not only to the mind, but also to the heart. That's why those songs of childhood remain with us throughout life, long after other textbook matters have faded without a trace. I'm very pleased that many of our new praise choruses tend toward the direct repetition of Scripture verses, because I'm convinced that in time, a new generation of believers will have God's Word engraved in their souls through these songs. A future with so much Scripture within us is a happy thought. Andrew Fletcher said, "Give me the making of the songs of a nation, and I care not who makes its laws."[2] We are not only what we eat, but what we sing.

It surprises me sometimes that parents pay so little attention to the lyrics their children are listening to. The words may be difficult to understand, but they're present in the songs. And even if your kids are not paying attention, those words are taking root subliminally. The songs are like Trojan horses, rolled up to the gates of the soul to smuggle in all kinds of godless influences. While we may not think we're taking in the lyrics, our minds are always busy with work that passes beneath the personal radar. Ask the gurus of Madison Avenue about the power of repeated words and phrases. They affect what we buy and what we believe.

ISRAEL'S GREATEST HITS

Everyone should take some time to read the great songs of the Bible; they'll be surprised to find how much music fills our Scripture. At key moments in their history, the Israelites created songs to commemorate the great works of God. And the inspired recorders of Scripture preserved these for us. They must have considered the songs not frivolous, but eternally important.

Here is an anthology of Israel's Greatest Hits through its "recorded" history:

- *There was a song of worship* after the Israelites had passed through the Red Sea (see Exodus 15:1-21). The Egyptians were routed, the Jews were safe, and Moses sat down to compose a song of triumph and praise.
- *There was a song of worship* when Deborah led the Israelites in victory over Jabin, king of Canaan (see Judges 5). She was a female

93

military commander, and the first female songwriter introduced in the Bible.

- *There was a song of worship* when David returned and enshrined the ark in Jerusalem (see 1 Chronicles 15:16, 27–28; 16:4–7). We're told that he personally took charge of the musical celebration, appointing singers and instrumentalists. David also wrote a lengthy psalm for the occasion and placed it in the hands of Asaph, his "music minister." You'll find it in complete form in 1 Chronicles 16:8–36—a jubilant song of praise.

- *There was a song of worship* at the coronation of King Solomon (see 1 Kings 1:39–40). It is said that the earth shook with the commotion of the people when they sang praises to God for giving them a new king.

- *There was a song of worship* when Solomon dedicated the temple of the Lord (see 1 Chronicles 23:5; 2 Chronicles 5:11–14). Take some time to let this fact sink in: A four-thousand-voice choir was accompanied by 120 trumpets. If four thousand choir members showed up to sing in my church, we'd have to take out all the pews; there would be no room for the regular congregation. The praise and worship were so powerful on the day of the temple dedication that a cloud actually moved through the interior of the massive building over the heads of the people. That cloud was the visible presence of God's glory. Wouldn't you like to be present for something so glorious?

- *There was a song of worship* when Nehemiah rebuilt the walls of the city of Jerusalem (see Nehemiah 12:27). It was a true day of victory. Against all odds and much opposition, a small but dedicated band of Israelites had rebuilt the ruined remnants of the city walls. Long-dead Jerusalem had risen from the ashes! Great music and celebration commemorated the occasion. Read this chapter and you'll see the intricate worship program that was planned.

- *There was a song of worship* during the revival led by Ezra after the wall was completed (see Nehemiah 12:45–47). As D. L. Moody once observed, music is just as important as preaching—sometimes far more—in impressing the Word of God upon people. Upon each of these defining moments of Israel's history, music was used to help the people see the "big picture" of what God was doing in their lives.

- *There was a song of worship* when the temple was rebuilt and rededicated under Zerubbabel and Ezra (see Ezra 2:41, 65; 3:10–13). Zerubbabel led the people home, Nehemiah rebuilt the city walls, and Ezra rebuilt the temple itself. We read that men and women were appointed as singers to lead the celebration. There were old men and women who could remember what the temple had looked like before its destruction. Now they beheld its resurrection, and they wept tears of almost unbelieving joy as they sang. Imagine the music of weeping and the shouts of joy, all intermingled and all acceptable to God as pure worship because it was given for His glory.

  The temple would fall into disgrace again, of course. Roman soldiers overran it and sealed the walls in A.D. 70, just as Jesus had foretold. History records that the singers and musicians refused to step down on that horrible day. They continued making a joyful noise unto the Lord as the soldiers attacked and martyred them— true worship indeed. We also know that the early Christians knelt and sang hymns in the center of the Coliseum as the Romans executed them.

- *There was a song of worship* when Jehoshaphat led his people

95

against Moab and Ammon (see 2 Chronicles 20:21–28). This passage tells us the singers were appointed to "praise the beauty of holiness" (v. 21). God responded to their music by delivering a great victory on the battlefield.

There are many other occasions when music takes center stage in Israel's epic narrative. Read for yourself. But perhaps it's less important for us to identify all the songs than to learn from them. What does the song of the ancients teach us about praising God?

Responding to God

In more than one hundred references in the Psalms, worshipers sang to the Lord. More than twenty passages speak of ministry to the Lord. The people came "before God" to praise Him. One hundred different passages describe the worshiper as "approaching" or "appearing" before God. In worship, we come into His presence—that much is clear. And how can we help but sing?

God instructed Moses in the building of the tabernacle. He said it would be a place to meet with His people and speak to them, to dwell among them and be their God. The word *tabernacle* actually means "rendezvous" or "appointment." When we come into the Lord's house, we are there for a rendezvous with the Almighty, a divine appointment. That should open our eyes. It should cause us to feel emotion and, finally, to sing.

I've talked to pastors of churches where the president came to worship when he visited that city. On such an occasion, believe me, a thrill passes through the congregation. No one sleeps late that day because it's a little rainy. Everyone rises early and puts on their finest suits and dresses—what else, for the most powerful man in the free world will be among them! The pastor somehow preaches a little better than his best. The choir sings as they've never sung before. The congregation is electric in its intensity. Even the pulpit and the windows seem shined to perfection.

We respect the office of the presidency. But should our response be any less when the Creator of the universe is among us? He is our most faithful attender. We forget that, don't we? We so easily lose sight of the fact that these aren't merely songs we're singing—they're songs offered *to God*. This is no mere meeting; it's a rendezvous with the Alpha and the Omega, the great I AM. If this is a place of divine appointment—and it is—we are standing on holy ground. We speak today of what we "got from" the service, whether or not we were "fed." And we think that's fairly pious and spiritual. Yet no one in Old Testament times thought of coming to worship to "get something out of it" or to have a "feel-good" experience. They understood, better than we do, that the essence of worship is giving. As we saw in the previous chapter, sacrifice is at the very center. We're not here to meet "felt needs," but to serve God, because it is right.

Worship is a response to God. Our choirs fall into the trap of "playing to the audience"; we preachers carefully work the crowd. But we're all playing to an audience of One—nothing else really matters. We worship together, but we should worship in one laser-focused direction, all but forgetful of those who sit beside us, those who listen to us, and those who sing for us. If our attention isn't directed above the steeple, our songs and prayers will never rise there. "I will praise the name of God with a song, and will magnify Him with thanksgiving. This also shall please the LORD better than an ox or bull" (Psalms 69:30–31).

REFLECTING OUR FAITH

Have you ever considered this point? Your music is a leading indicator of your spiritual life.

If a picture is worth a thousand words, your song is worth several thousand. It captures the state of your spirit at a given moment. It's not a matter, of course, of your melodic precision; it's all about the reflection of your soul.

We've observed plenty about Israel's more joyful celebrations, but not every moment was a mountaintop. Psalm 137 gives us a picture of the music that gives way to misery. The Israelites had more than their share of faith valleys. After a long period of disobedience, they served a sentence of captivity in Babylon. During that time, their captors mocked them. "We hear you Jews are talented singers," they jeered. "We don't hear any music—why don't you sing us a song?"

It's all recorded for us in Psalm 137. Here we are reminded that there are times when the spirit isn't given to music and laughter:

> By the rivers of Babylon,
> There we sat down, yea, we wept
> When we remembered Zion.
> We hung our harps
> Upon the willows in the midst of it.
> For there those who carried us away captive asked of us a song,
> And those who plundered us requested mirth,
> Saying, "Sing us one of the songs of Zion!"
> How shall we sing the LORD's song
> In a foreign land?
>
> —PSALM 137:1–4

How can there be music in so hellish a place? How could we think of singing? Such times have their own sad melodies and musical forms. There are songs of oppression. We find these, too, among the psalms.

98

Whether joy or sadness, our songs are our spiritual barometer. What is your reading today? Is there within your heart a melody, or are you singing the blues? Does your song need to be, "Oh, God, restore unto me the joy of my salvation"?

What is true for the individual is true for the congregation. Perhaps you've visited a few churches and noted the intangible differences. You can feel it within a moment of crossing the sanctuary threshold. The pipe organ may be magnificent, the choir may be a multitude, but if the Spirit of God is not in that place, you can feel the emptiness.

Then again, you might enter a place of worship with precisely the opposite atmosphere. It could be a new church meeting in a run-down school gym, and the worship leader may be twanging a guitar that has been out of tune since the early sixties. But if God is there, you sense it immediately. You could almost cut the ambient joy with a knife, and the singing is heartfelt.

Spiritually sensitive people can detect the difference just by an intuitive sense—a kind of inner "divining rod," if you will—but almost anyone can tell by the music. It measures out our faith, note by note.

RELEASING THE WHOLE PERSON

As a student in seminary I was thrilled to attend one of the greatest churches in America. For several months I was a part of First Baptist Church of Dallas, Texas, when the legendary Dr. W. A. Criswell was pastor. Those weeks left a great mark on all the ministry that has followed for me. The worship there placed me in God's presence week after week. But one practice in particular totally captivated me.

My wife and I were in the balcony on our first Sunday at First Baptist. The time for the pastoral prayer arrived, and the men who were seated on the platform all rose as one. Together they walked to the front of the platform and knelt. There were microphones placed across the front of the platform so whoever happened to be praying could lead the congregation from his knees. But that wasn't what amazed me at the time. As I watched, the congregation reached forward, without prompting, and pulled out the kneeling benches installed in the pews before them. All God's people fell to their knees together and joined in prayer to God.

To me, this was the Eighth Wonder of the World. I had never seen that level of congregational worship involvement. It changed my thinking on a lot of things, and the impact remains with me to this very day. As we read through the testimony of worship throughout the Old Testament, we don't find folks leaning back against comfy pew cushions, hoping to stay awake. We find people totally involved from a bodily perspective: They sing, they shout, they mourn, they lift hands, they kneel down, and they fall on their faces.

Consider your last visit to a big sporting event. How did the crowd behave? Did you see a lot of chins resting wearily on fists? Was anyone dozing off? I suspect you saw something more like this: people leaping to their feet; people shouting, cheering, booing, and expressing derision at times; people clapping, cheering, singing, stomping. All of this is because these "true believers" have hearts and minds captivated by their team—there's no way their bodies aren't going to get into the act, for the body always takes its cue from the heart and mind.

I certainly don't recommend that we bring the rowdiness of the professional sporting arena to modern worship; I especially don't want anyone booing the choir or shouting derision during the sermon, and I'd hate to see "the wave" break out across the sanctuary. But I do recognize that music is a channel for the wonder of worship. It brings the music of the angels to our everyday existence. Isn't it wonderful that you could be on your hands and knees, scrubbing a filthy floor and singing the music of Zion?

Music helps you transport your spirit from mundane corners to majestic splendor. The body follows where the heart leads—and vice versa, as a matter of fact. Your prayers will be more focused and your mind more alert if you've aligned yourself on your knees. Some of your best worship might occur when you're jogging or driving a car, when your body is tensed to the task. Do you want to know how to incorporate worship into every moment of your day? Music is an excellent place to start.

Let's sing unto the Lord because it's one more way to give our bodies to His praises. Let's sing because music expresses levels of adoration we can't find in the spoken word. Let's sing because the people of the world will be attracted to our music. And let's sing because we absolutely can't help it! Our Lord reigns!

9

Let Heaven and Nature Sing

NINE

Let Heaven and Nature Sing

I HEARD OF A FARMER who was making his regular visit to the big city to stock up on supplies. Only this time, for one reason or another, necessity kept the farmer in town over the weekend. So he decided to find a church for his Sunday worship.

Back home this farmer attended a little wood-frame church where the preaching was energetic and the songs were of the old-time gospel variety. But on his weekend trip, the farmer decided it was time to gain a bit more experience of the religious world. So on Sunday morning he walked into a stately edifice with massive columns and a ceiling higher than any grain silo he'd ever seen. This, he concluded, was where they had "high church" meetings, as he'd heard them called. The farmer found a seat and worshiped the best he knew how, even though it seemed like he was in the "advanced" course and he was used to the "beginner" level.

When he arrived home at the farm, he regaled his wife with an account of his visit to the "advanced" worship service. She listened with fascination; it was as if her husband had been to the Land of Oz. "The singin'," she demanded. "What was the singin' like?"

"Anthems," her husband replied. "We sang us some anthems."

"And what, pray tell, is an anthem?"

The farmer stroked his beard pensively. Well," he replied slowly, "I can't rightly describe 'em, but it's a little like this. If I was to say to you, 'Bessie Mae, it's time to feed the pigs,' that would *not* be an anthem. No, ma'am. But if I was to put it to you, 'Bessie, Bessie, Bessie Mae, Bessie Mae, it's time; Bessie Mae, it's time to feed, it's time, it's time to feed; it's time to feed the pigs, the pigs, it's time to feed the pigs, pigs, pigs, Amen!'—well now, as I understand it, that's what you call an *anthem.*"

It's true that we have our various musical idioms. The way we sing in my church bears very little resemblance to the way a church sings in Japan or Argentina. And we have very little idea how the first Christians expressed their melodies. What matters is that we are a singing people, nearly everywhere. A famous atheist named Robert Ingersoll left explicit instructions for his funeral: "There will be no singing."[1] And I can understand that; what is there to sing about if the heavenly throne is empty? But if our faith is valid, as our hearts tell us it is, then we of all people can sing—regardless of our ability to join the Three Sopranos onstage. John Wesley once said, "Beware of singing as if you were half-dead or half-asleep. Lift up your voices with strength. Be no more afraid of your voice now, or more ashamed of its being heard, than when you sang the songs of Satan."[2]

Yet I know many people who don't like to sing. I can see them from the pulpit, barely moving their lips as if they're afraid the hymn might escape captivity. Or they shift from one foot to the other, watching everyone else and checking their watches occasionally. If I were to embarrass my nonsinging friend by asking him about it, I can anticipate his reply: "Oh, pastor, you haven't heard how poorly I sing. The Bible says 'make a joyful noise,' and I have the 'noise' part covered—but my singing sounds like an injured moose!"

The problem with that reasoning is that my friend isn't singing for me. He isn't singing for the people surrounding him in the pews. He sings for the pleasure of God, who accepts gifts based on the heart, not the craftsmanship. If you have a range of one note, that note is all the more beautiful in the ears of the Lord, if it's offered up to Him. The *joyfulness* of the joyful noise isn't determined by the social evaluation of your instrument, but by the divine evaluation of your heart.

True worship puts the song within you and leaves it in place throughout the week. It may find full voice in the sanctuary of the church, but the melody lingers on as you move through the hours of the workday, as you spend time with your family, as you thank the Lord for another safe and fruitful day and drift off to sleep. I know many people who exercise with praise music in their earphones and on their hearts, and they even say it gives them a second wind as they jog or go about their aerobic routine. It's a shame that so few families still sing together. There was a time when "hymn sings" were important features of family reunions. Music helped tie families together, and the content of the music was the greatness of God.

"I will sing with the spirit, and I will also sing with the understanding" (1 Corinthians 14:15b). When we immerse our hearts and minds in the music of worship, life changes radically. Why go about our business with a television commercial jingle on our minds when we can be bathing our minds with the Word itself, in musical form? Why face the trials of business with anything but songs of our awesome God on your tongue?

"You are my hiding place; you shall preserve me from trouble; you shall surround me with songs of deliverance" (Psalms 32:7).

My Heart's Desire

Something to Sing About

Music, after all, is amazing. Studies seem to indicate that your potted plant grows more rapidly and robustly if Mozart is playing in the room. Can you doubt that you, who are created in the very image of God, will grow more like Him, and more quickly, when His melodies and His truth are the soundtrack to your life? God gave potted plants no lips for singing, but He gave you that ability—whether you have operatic talent or can only squawk like a bird. And He's given you plenty to sing about. Let's examine some of the reasons for singing, as set out for us in Ephesians 5:18–21 and the parallel passage, Colossians 3:16:

> And do not be drunk with wine, in which is dissipation; but be filled with the Spirit, speaking to one another in psalms and hymns and spiritual songs, singing and making melody in your heart to the Lord, giving thanks always for all things to God the Father in the name of our Lord Jesus Christ, submitting to one another in the fear of God.
>
> —EPHESIANS 5:18–21

This incredible passage is itself music to our ears. It suggests several reasons your throat should be filled with praise.

We Sing Because His Spirit Fills Us

There have been many things said about what happens when we're filled with the Spirit—many odd and controversial things, as a matter of fact. But the Word of God says that when the Spirit of God comes among us, we begin to sing. We admonish one another with psalms and hymns and spiritual songs. The true song of worship is born first of all out of this truth: God's Holy Spirit has come to live within His children. We tune our hearts to sing His praise because He is the One who does the fine-tuning.

This is the very validation that God is among us. Martin Luther once wrote, "The devil hates music because he can't stand gaiety. Satan can smirk but he can't laugh; he can sneer but he can't sing."[3] Perhaps Luther was thinking of this amazing verse: "Then our mouth was filled with laughter, and our tongue with singing. Then they said among the nations, 'The LORD has done great things for them'" (Psalms 126:2). If you were an outsider among a new group of people, what would attract you most to them? Perhaps it would be the twin glories of music and laughter that mark any family of kindred souls. Uplifting music and hearty—not derisive—laughter are signs that truly God has done great things for us. The world can't resist such joy. Perhaps the church is losing its influence with the world because we're seldom perceived as having a sense of humor or hearts filled with spirited music.

But at our best, we can be found singing hymns of praise at funerals. Who else could face death with hope but God's own children? Our music doesn't arise from our circumstances; it embodies the hope with which we face them.

There was once a great singer, composer, and song leader named Ira Sankey. As George Beverly Shea has served the ministry of Billy Graham, so did Sankey serve the evangelist D. L. Moody. They traveled everywhere together, preaching and singing about Jesus Christ. But during his final five years of life, Sankey lost both his eyesight and his singing ability. Ill health confined him to a small apartment. He was very near to death.

One day F. B. Meyer came to Ira Sankey on a mission of encouragement. The two men sat, relived the wonderful past they shared, and reminisced about precious memories. Crowds had been galvanized and the Spirit of God released as Sankey would sing, Moody would preach, and Meyer would teach. What a team, and how many mighty works of God they had witnessed! Those had been the days.

After a great while, they fell silent and Meyer said to his friend, "My brother, would you sing for me once more?" It was a startling request of an ailing old man. But Meyer gently led his friend over to a melodeon within the apartment. Sankey sat at the keyboard and lifted his shaky, shrunken fingers. Then, hesitantly at first, he began to play a beloved old melody. Then he opened his mouth and released a song from the tired remnants of his vocal cords.

There was certainly no beauty about it as the world counts beauty. Perhaps the old pipes had a leak or two. But F. B. Meyer, the great Christian teacher and writer, began to weep like a baby. "There'll be no dark valley when Jesus comes," Sankey struggled to sing.

And sure enough, it was only a few days later that Sankey awoke in the eternal morning of the presence of Jesus. When he awoke, he could sing as he never had before. And his eyes, once a dim mirror, could now see God face to face.[4]

That's the nature of our hope and joy. It's what enables us to sing. It's also why the precision of our singing is irrelevant. Ira Sankey, from the darkness of his lost eyesight and the ruin of his once-gifted vocal instrument, could sing with joy and elation. The Spirit lives in our heart, is undiminished by time or health, and gives us joy to the last.

WE SING BECAUSE HIS WORD INDWELLS US

Our passage from Ephesians has a near-mirror image in the Book of Colossians. It goes like this: "Let the word of Christ dwell in you richly in all wisdom, teaching and admonishing one another in psalms and hymns and spiritual songs, singing with grace in your hearts to the Lord" (Colossians 3:16). This verse is very similar, but it adds significantly to our understanding of a lifestyle of worship.

Ephesians points to our being filled with the Spirit, Colossians to our being filled with the Word of God, which dwells within us richly. Then, by psalms and hymns and spiritual songs, we partake in wisdom and teaching together. Combine the two passages and we see a melody and countermelody of being filled with God's Word and God's Spirit, responding with beautiful music in both cases.

We need both of these, the Spirit and the Word, to be Christians. Subtract either and it's simply not possible. One reshapes the heart and the other the mind, and together they make us whole persons molded to the image of Christ. The Word of God provides the content; the Spirit of God applies it. He impresses the teachings of the Scriptures upon us, applies them to us, and reminds us of them at need. All the great, enduring hymns and songs of worship are drawn from God's Word. Throughout time, many believers have been inspired to create hymns as they've read God's Word. Very often, they've told us they were convinced that God gave them the melody as well. How could powerful songs like "Amazing Grace" and "Joy to the World" have any other source but God? They have thrilled and inspired generation upon generation.

WE SING FOR THE RICH DIVERSITY OF THE EXPERIENCE

It's ironic, as we shall see, that there is so much controversy today over what kind of music is fit for worship. Should we sing the old hymns? Should we sing the new songs? Should we sing directly from the psalms? Which is appropriate?

The answer is . . . yes!

Paul tells us to sing psalms and hymns and spiritual songs. That about covers it. In the earliest days of the church there was great diversity in the music, just as there was great diversity among the believers. People brought music from their various cultural backgrounds and baptized it in the transforming Word of God through His Spirit. They sang psalms, hymns, and spiritual songs. What are the meanings of these terms? Let's examine them closely.

Paul first mentions *psalms*. These were the psalms we still have in the center of our Bibles and in a few other places where the beloved anthems of the Israelites were found, from Moses' song of deliverance to the great poetry of the prophets. Jesus knew them by heart and quoted them frequently.

But we are also to praise the Lord with *hymns*. These were new forms of musical expression bursting from the grateful hearts of the early Christians. Nearly all biblical scholars agree that Philippians 2:5–11 is a beautiful example of an early church hymn. Paul was writing about the incarnation of Jesus, God becoming man, and there were no better words for it than those he found in the hymn. Since hymns were cleverly used to summarize crucial Christian doctrines, it's likely that many passages in the New Testament were actually hymns. Revelation 4:11 ("You are worthy, O Lord, to receive glory and honor and power . . .") may have been a hymn that perfectly expressed what John wanted to say.

We've never stopped writing hymns throughout two thousand years of Christian history. Fanny Crosby, a blind woman, wrote two thousand of them. Charles Wesley wrote another eight thousand. Many have heard the story of John Newton, who barely survived a terrible storm off the northwest coast of Ireland. God answered his desperate, terrified prayers, and he responded by writing what is probably the most beloved song in all Christendom:

Amazing grace, how sweet the sound
That saved a wretch like me,
I once was lost, but now am found,
Was blind, but now I see!

What would we do without "Amazing Grace" or so many more of our great hymns? There are some of them written by men and women whose lives we know almost nothing about, yet their work is still ministering, still touching hearts, hundreds of years after the human composers have passed into obscurity. Few human instruments have been so thoroughly used by God's Spirit as hymns.

Finally, what of the *spiritual songs?* Here, we find, most of the controversy originates. The words are translated literally as "ode to a breath." The idea is something rushing spontaneously from the spirit. We can imagine that worship services of the early church were much less formal than our services today. As a matter of fact, Paul, in some of his letters, actually calls for a bit more orderliness. If you and I had visited a service in the first century, we might have seen someone stand spontaneously and sing a solo. As he finished, someone else might have stood to recite a beloved verse from the Hebrew Scriptures. Nearly everyone probably took part in spontaneity of worship. The phrase *spiritual songs* may allude to singing to God in a way that was as natural and spontaneous as breathing, an ode to a breath—but it also covers all the beautiful music we've used for praising God over the years.

The gospel, from the very beginning, is about freedom—freedom not only from the bondage of sin, but also from the reliance on priests; freedom from the dry legalism of the law; freedom from the barriers between Jew and Gentile. As such, there was a new diversity that the early believers found refreshing and exciting. We can be diverse in our worship styles today, blending time-honored Handel and modern praise choruses. All of it is acceptable to the Lord, as long as we offer it with the right heart. We ourselves are diverse, representing every age group, cultural background, gender, and outlook. Our music and expression will reflect that. Hymns tend to tether us to our tradition—not at all a bad thing; spiritual songs allow us to speak to the moment, a good thing as well. The latter tend not to endure as well as hymns, but they serve a dynamic purpose within the cultural moment.

Hymns that seem "formal and churchy" to us might surprise us by their origins. Martin Luther and others actually took common everyday melodies and redeemed them with the truth of God's Word. We must always be willing to wrap the age-old truths in the best of brand-new packages.

Imagine the church on this corner of the street that sings only new songs. Across the street, imagine the church that adheres to the hymns. And then, on this third corner, is the church that specializes in spiritual songs. On Sunday morning, you can stand at the intersection and hear all the music intermingle—to our ears chaos and cacophony; but as it rises to heaven, all of it miraculously interweaves until it becomes a beautiful harmony in the ears of the Lord, for so many different people are worshiping. We have no need to limit ourselves if God Himself doesn't do so. Paul didn't advise "psalms *or* hymns *or* spiritual songs." He used the word *and*—a word that means *diversity.*

We Sing to Rejoice

William Cowper (1731–1800) was no older than six when he watched his mother die. His father, unable to care for him, sent the boy away to a boarding school. The youngest and smallest boy there, young William became the subject of a good bit of bullying and persecution. He was beaten and ridiculed until he despaired for his very life.

As young Cowper grew a bit older, two failed love relationships left him brokenhearted. He tried several times to take his own life, including an overdose of opium as well as hanging and an attempt to fall upon the blade of his own knife—which broke beneath him. As a matter of fact, each time he attempted suicide, he was spared by some strange twist of fate. Not that it seemed to matter; he was a miserable, empty individual who saw no more purpose for living. Mental illness grew until he was shut away in an asylum. And it was there, in the lowest and most miserable of all places for that time period, that the Lord finally caught up with William Cowper.

It happened on the day when Cowper was being visited by a relative who opened a Bible and shared Romans 3:25. The relative patiently began explaining the meaning of these mysterious ideas of propitiation, faith, and blood. Jesus, through His own suffering and persecution, had come to redeem everything dark, everything miserable in this world. He, too, had been despised and rejected by men. But His love overcame everything. It reached even now across the ages, through the expanses, down to the depths of a mental asylum and into this tortured soul.

It was, Cowper would later explain, the first time the eyes of his soul had beheld a ray of hope. Jesus cared for him. Jesus had covered all the transgressions of his life and blotted them out with His own blood. Surely it was Jesus who had broken the blade of the knife, who had kept him from hanging, who had on one evening used a fog to keep him from finding a river and throwing himself into it. With a heart full of joy, William Cowper became a follower of Christ that day. Even before he was released from the asylum, the happy young man took pen in hand and composed these words:

There is a fountain filled with blood
Drawn from Immanuel's veins,
And sinners plunged beneath that flood
Lose all their guilty stains.

William Cowper had found the right river for immersing himself, and misery gave way to melody. The depths of his suffering, once no more than emptiness, were now miraculously transformed to wisdom, poetry, and majestic strains of music. Great hymns poured out of his former pain. God had restrained him from taking his own life and then turned all his suffering into something that could touch the world. In response, Cowper wrote, "God moves in a mysterious way, His wonders to perform."[5]

Best of all, that same kind of supernatural intervention still happens. You can ask Christian songwriter and worship leader Don Moen about that. Late at night in a remote part of the Texas panhandle, his wife's sister and her husband were traveling with their four children. They never saw the approaching truck, and its driver never saw them. The children were thrown from the van.

In the terrible darkness, the parents followed the sounds of crying to their wounded children. But Craig Phelps's nine-year-old son wasn't crying. His neck was broken upon impact, and he was dead.

Craig, a doctor, quickly tried to revive his son. But God's voice cut through the chaos: *Jeremy is with Me,* God seemed to say. *You deal with those who are living.* It took forty-five excruciating minutes for the ambulance to arrive at this desolate little patch of wilderness.

The next day, on his way to the funeral by plane, Don Moen opened his Bible. Was it merely chance that directed his eyes to Isaiah 43:19? I think not. "I will even make a road in the wilderness," Don read, "and rivers in the desert." A song immediately welled up within him, as if fully formed. It was one of those moments when divine inspiration overpowers an artist.

After the mournful service, Don embraced the bereaved parents; their tears mingled with his own. He managed to tell them that God had provided a song especially for them. And with a lump in his throat, he somehow sang:

> God will make a way where there seems to be no way,
> He works in ways we cannot see.
> He will make a way for me.
> He will be my guide, hold me closely to His side,
> With love and strength for each new day,
> He will make a way, He will make a way.
>
> By a road in the wilderness He'll lead me,
> And rivers in the desert will I see;
> Heaven and earth will fade,
> But His Word will still remain,
> He will do something new today.

Today, that little song has made its way around the world. It offers the comfort of the Lord in every corner of the globe, simply because God's grieving children made a way to worship in the worst of life's wilderness. They could have fixed their eyes on the wreckage of a wilderness road, but they saw instead the invisible road—the one God always provides toward hope and deliverance. The Phelpses and the Moens knew that at the end of that road, a laughing nine-year-old waits to welcome them.[6]

Make no mistake about it: Music is a special channel of divine blessing, comfort, and strength. Even in the depths of suffering, we can turn our hearts and voices to lovely music provided by the hand of God. Someday we'll stand before the throne, singing and proclaiming all our praises to the King, with all the eloquence we've dreamed of having. For now, set within this earthly realm, we have music to give us a preview, a foretaste of glory divine. Music is a precious gift from God, planted in the grounds of our souls, then liberated by our lips to return to its heavenly home.

God will always make a way, and one of the clearest and straightest roads to Him is the music He gives us.

10

This Means War!

TEN

This Means War!

I T WAS ONE OF THOSE BEAUTIFUL TWILIGHTS in mid-March when a dark mood is impossible. The wind was soft, the air was cool, and it was a joy simply to stand under the sky and watch the first twinkle of distant stars.

The city was San Francisco, and the man's name was Jerry Brandt. Jerry leads a group called Action Evangelism, and his passion is the big city. An outdoor praise and prayer service was scheduled for Union Square on this lovely evening. The event would kick off a new initiative to reach out to the city's homeless.

Jerry arrived early to tend to some of the details. But as he made his way to Union Park, there was trouble. A mob suddenly turned the corner and came hurrying down Market Street. Jerry had gone through the right channels to reserve this park. He had signed the papers and handled all the red tape—officially at least. But this crowd wasn't too concerned about papers and permissions. They had an agenda of their own, and they were eager to tell Jerry about it. A man stepped out in front of the pack and demanded, "Are you in charge here?"

Jerry hadn't been prepared for this development. He took a deep breath and replied, "Second in command. Jesus Christ is the One in charge."

The man, of course, paid no attention to his answer. He was already gesturing toward Market Street and the small army that flanked him.

"We have a thousand people heading this way," he challenged. "We're taking this place over. Just wait until the rest of us arrive."

There wasn't a lot of time for deliberation on Jerry's part. What had been planned as a positive event—a worship service, no less—now looked as if it could quickly turn ugly, even dangerous. What would you have said? What would you have done?

Jerry didn't have to reflect more than an instant. Immediately he felt a tug at his heart. God provided the words, and Jerry delivered them with confidence: "Let me tell you something," he said. "You're too late. Jesus has already taken over this square, and we're going to lift up His name right here tonight."

About fifteen of Jerry's people were present. He gathered them together and prayed immediately for the rest of the group to arrive. Then Jerry and his friends stepped up to the platform and continued with their preparations. Their business was worship and praise, nothing more or less—God could see to the rest. As the volunteers worked, a member of the crew shared a verse from the Scriptures. It was Deuteronomy 28:7, which reads, "The LORD will cause your enemies who rise against you to be defeated before your face; they shall come out against you one way and flee before you seven ways." Power somehow came through that little verse. It was a promise claimed, a shot of adrenaline, a battle cry; everyone was filled with new strength and courage. Jerry and his friends knew it was only a matter of ignoring the threats that had been hurled at them—then worshiping and praising God's name.

Suddenly, however, their eyes were drawn to a startling sight. At the entrance to the square, the angry army had halted in their tracks. Now they were performing an about-face and rushing away from Union Square. They were flowing out as rapidly as they had surged in, but now motivated by some different emotion—something that bore a passing resemblance to fear. The praises of God had scattered them and cleared the battlefield.

"Looking back on that night," Jerry tells us, "we realized it was God who delivered us. And He did it entirely through the power of praise." The incident changed Jerry's ministry forever. As his friends work in the streets and find themselves in the grips of spiritual warfare, the first thing they do is to begin praising and worshiping God.[1]

Worship is the weapon that turns the battle every time.

THE POWER OF PRAISE

Most of us are familiar with the idea of praise as worship. Some of us are comfortable with the concept of praise as a witness. But few of us have tapped the surprising power of praise as a weapon of warfare. In confrontation, our first impulse is to become defensive. But here is one way we can seize the offensive: Simply lift up and exalt the name of the Lord God.

Worship and warfare? Perhaps you might have identified those as enemies rather than comrades. But I didn't invent this idea; the Bible has been filled with it all along. Skim your Old Testament—start with the Book of Joshua—and you'll find the people of God constantly riding into battle, praising God's name as they go. You'll also find the times when they fought with no hearts for worship, and on those occasions they were routed. Victorious warfare always required victorious worship. And my question is, Why should things be any different today?

We modern believers are quick to discuss warfare (spiritual or otherwise), and we have strong opinions about worship. But we seldom make the crucial connection between the two. We will never go into battle without the proper worship of God's name. Our failure to grasp that idea may account for more problems in modern Christianity than we're ready to consider. The fact is that praise and worship are *refining* processes. We can't be in God's presence without a deep awareness of our sin and without confessing and allowing the purification that only He can provide. Worship cleanses our hands and hearts, and then we can see how to fight. Then we can clear the sinful mists from our eyes and do things God's way.

Some have said that Satan has an allergic reaction whenever there is true worship. That's an interesting way of visualizing it; perhaps when we break out in praise, the devil breaks out in hives. I don't know whether he itches, sneezes, or coughs, but I do know he becomes very uncomfortable on those occasions when we take our eyes off ourselves and place them squarely and worshipfully on the Lord of grace. That's when God's mighty works finally come to pass. That's when we take powerful weapons in hand, crying, "Onward, Christian soldiers!" and advancing on the enemy's holdings. The forces of hell cannot prevail against the uplifted name of Christ.

A Little Dab of Devil-Be-Gone

Mary Slosser, the prominent missionary in China, once said that when she found herself in the midst of demonic activity and worldly pressures, she would sing the Doxology and dismiss the devil. That expresses the idea with a certain snap, doesn't it? Praise is a powerful weapon. Amy Carmichael, a missionary who cared for children in South India, added,

"I believe truly that Satan cannot endure praise and worship, so he slips out of the room, more or less, when there is a true song."[2] And evangelist Jack Taylor wrote, "The liars from the pit of hell cannot market their wares in an atmosphere of praise and worship."[3]

Those are three voices from the not-so-distant past. But let's listen to one from a bit further back—a man named Ignatius of Antioch. He lived only eighty years after Jesus' resurrection and wrote a book called *The Epistle to the Ephesians,* though I need not tell you it's not the same epistle in our Bibles. Ignatius wrote:

> Take heed, then, often to come together to give thanks to God and show forth his praise, for when ye come frequently together in the same place, the powers of Satan are destroyed and his fiery darts urging to sin, fall back ineffectual. For your concord and harmonious faith prove his destruction, and the torment of his assistants.[3]

Did you know there is someone who really gets bent out of shape whenever you go to church? No, not that fellow in the next pew who objects to your singing. It truly torments the devil and every one of his "assistants" when you worship God, in the public sanctuary or the private one. It throws a wrench into the detailed agenda of demonic works. In all the other things we do, from watching television to grocery shopping to taking business trips, there are countless windows of opportunity for the devil to steal in and do his thing. But when you worship God devotedly, Satan is out of his league. He is completely stripped of power, and that's always been the one thing the devil can't abide.

Worship has always been our weapon. Consider that midnight in a Philippian jail, when two prisoners named Paul and Silas lifted their voices and sang praises to God. Consider Jonah, the hapless prophet-become-fish-food, singing a song of praise and deliverance to the God who placed him in a whale's belly. If it made the fish vomit, you can imagine how much more allergic the devil is to praise songs rising above the sounds of battle. Think of all the psalms in which David begins in deep depression, lamenting the injustice of his enemies' success. In so many of these, he turns his attention and poetry to the praises of God, and his psalm finishes on a note of victory.

That can become the pattern of your life.

The Heart of the Battle

In 2 Chronicles we find the story of a troubled time in the country of Judah. This was a dark period that served as a counterpoint to the magnificent reigns of David and Solomon. The nation had become divided against itself, then two smaller countries of Israel in the north and Judah in the south. Israel was ruled by an evil king named Ahab, along with his equally wicked wife, Jezebel. They were the ultimate ancient "power couple," icons of corrupt government.

But to the south, the nation of Judah was ruled by a far more benevolent monarch. His name was Jehoshaphat, the fourth king of Judah. The Scriptures tell us that he walked in the ways of the Lord and honored the traditions of David. So there was an evil northern king and a righteous southern one. But in time the two nations were united politically through a marriage alliance, when Ahab's daughter married Jehoshaphat's son.

As it happened, Ahab tried to use that alliance to manipulate his southern counterpart. He courted Jehoshaphat, wining and dining him until the southern king agreed to join his nation in a war against one of Israel's enemies. Jehoshaphat knew he was doing something unwise; a prophet had warned him against unholy alliances. Ill-advised mergers, in marriage, business, or politics will destroy everything we've set out to accomplish. But Ahab was the father of Jehoshaphat's daughter-in-law. How could Jehoshaphat say no? He could have, but he didn't.

Together the forces of Israel and Judah rolled into warfare. We remember the great battle primarily because the arrow of some unnamed bowman found its mark, slipping between the chinks of Ahab's armor. Thus the evil king died in battle.

Jehoshaphat, however, lived to tell the story. More than that, he lived to reflect deeply upon its implications. The king knew that God's help in our battles is a reflection of how the Lord feels about our obedience. Jehoshaphat knew he had formed an alliance that grieved God deeply, and surely the king would have to pay for his ill-considered move. By God's grace his life hadn't been taken—yet. What should he do? How could he repent? He had compromised principles to please the father of his son's wife, but the result was that very man's death.

So Jehoshaphat came sadly to his own door at last, and who should meet him there but God's prophet? Jehu the seer was waiting for him, possibly the very last person the weary king wanted to see. The seer voiced the precise thought that already occupied Jehoshaphat's mind: "Should you help the wicked and love those who hate the LORD? Therefore the wrath of the LORD is upon you" (2 Chronicles 19:2). But he also affirmed that God wasn't entirely unpleased with Jehoshaphat's reign; the king had removed wooden idols and had a heart to seek God.

No doubt these vital signs of his devotion had saved Jehoshaphat's life. Now there could be a second chance, with no further disastrous deviations from the path God had set out for him—he would see to that. Jehoshaphat settled down and served the Lord with consistency and without compromise, as best he could.

MY HEART'S DESIRE

THE BATTLE FOR THE HEART

Life was fairly peaceful until the day when the messenger burst into the palace with grave news. An army was mobilizing along Judah's border, and it was a massive force. Attack was imminent.

Jehoshaphat had been in this position before, and he had learned one thing: The heart of the battle is the battle for the heart. Compromised devotion will not do. Had the king learned his lesson well? I've found in my own life that, when we fail the exam, God often gives a retest, and He often gives it promptly. Here was Jehoshaphat's retest, and he passed it with flying colors.

We find the account in 2 Chronicles 20. The attackers were the Ammonites and the Moabites, and they were joined by a third army from beyond the Dead Sea. This was a serious challenge with nothing less than the overthrow of Jehoshaphat as its goal. "And Jehoshaphat feared, and set himself to seek the LORD, and proclaimed a fast throughout all Judah. So Judah gathered together to ask help from the LORD; and from all the cities of Judah they came to seek the LORD" (2 Chronicles 20:3–4).

"And Jehoshaphat feared." Was there something wrong with the king for being afraid? There would have been something wrong with him if he *hadn't* feared. Fear is the recognition that we lack the resources for the challenge confronting us. Jehoshaphat knew his kingdom was overmatched from the military perspective. His hope lay not in the might of armies, but in the hand of God. That's why Jehoshaphat called all the people together for a national time of prayer and fasting. It was the king's first resort, not his last, to seek God in this crisis, and he saw that all his people did the same.

As we read the verses that follow, we find that Jehoshaphat stood before his people and took the lead in worshiping and praising God. He praised God for who He is. He praised Him for what He had done. Finally, he praised God for what He could do in the future. Then he turned his praise to petition, asking that God would indeed manifest His power on behalf of His people. "Here they come, these godless invaders," he was saying in so many words. "They have always been an affront to You and to Your people. We might have destroyed them when we came out of Egypt, but You restrained us then. Now they return, and they reward Your mercy with threats. They would take the land You've set apart—the land You gave us for our home. Will You not judge them?" He also acknowledged that the armies of Judah were powerless in the face of this threat and ignorant in how to respond. On behalf of his nation, Jehoshaphat threw himself upon the mercy of God.

We read that there was a sermon in this praise gathering, too. One of the prophets of the kingdom stood and preached, calling on everyone to put their trust in God. "Don't be afraid," he told them. "The battle isn't yours—the battle belongs to the Lord." Led by the king, everyone bowed before God and prayed. And the intriguing observation we make is that, woven throughout the sincere praise and worship of God—through the sermon, the singing, the supplication—the strategy for battle came together. Worship and warfare were intertwined in a way that we of the twenty-first century would never imagine if we didn't discover it here.

WORSHIP GOES TO WAR

The nation's gathering came to a close, but their worship didn't. The next day, the battle was taken up. The armies continued to worship as they faced down the enemy. This was an army that sang as they marched forward, "Praise the LORD, for His mercy endures forever!" This was all by design; Jehoshaphat appointed soldiers to sing and other soldiers to praise God "for the beauty of holiness" (2 Chronicles 20:21). The singers carried no weapons but their voices and their hearts of adoration. And as the people praised God's name and sang their hymns, the hand of the Lord began to move against the enemy, as verse 22 tells us. As a matter of fact, in the face of Judah's unified praise and devotion, the enemy basically consumed itself. The three invading armies turned upon one another in confusion and slaughtered themselves until no man was left standing.

So we see that just as battle plans were solidified through worship, so worship culminated on the battlefield. I believe there's a profound lesson for us to glean from this striking concept. When we go forth into the battle—whether we battle through a family crisis or a career problem—we have two strategies. We can go in our own weakness and face defeat, or we can take the power of the Lord with us.

How do we do the latter? We simply love, adore, worship, and praise His name. We know that God makes His home in our praises, and He will march with us even to the farthest corners of the earth and the end of the age. As we worship, our life strategies come together in ways we could never have formulated on our own. Then, as we face the challenges head-on, we keep right on praising, right on singing to the Lord, who is greater and stronger than any challenge that might stand in our path. The wonder of worship, guiding our everyday experiences, will totally change the way we see everything that confronts us, including issues of spiritual warfare.

What is that challenge for you today? I would urge you not to focus on the misery of the crisis, but on the mastery of Christ. Then follow Him into battle. See if the demons themselves don't turn and flee from the gateway, terrified by the sounds of godly praise and adoration.

11

Strange but True Worship Stories

ELEVEN

〜〜 *Strange But True Worship Stories* 〜〜

E'VE CONSIDERED THE STORY of Jehoshaphat, a king who won a battle through worship. It's not so hard for us to accept such a story; it comes from God's Word, after all, and it happened in distant Bible times. Miracles simply seemed a part of the fabric of everyday experience in those days.

But what about today? We often hear Christians shrug and say, "The great tide of miracles dried up when Bible times came to a close. This is the age of science; God doesn't do things like that anymore. Our miracles are technology and medicine."

I hope not! I often wonder how much of God's power for today we consign to the closed book of the past. Could it be that we have not because we ask not and that we see no miracles because we expect none? If you're dead set on the proposition that miracles don't happen in your life, I can guarantee you that you'll be right. But if you live your everyday life in the power of faith, expecting God to reach down into the most mundane of activities in the most modern of worlds, you may begin to see wonderful things.

There are people today who refuse to be ruled by conventional thought. They expect great things from God, and they attempt great things for God. They walk out to the edge of human limitations and take one more courageous step out into the frontier of faith, where there are no limits but the sovereign will of God. Medicine and megabytes are not enough for them; they live as if we serve a mighty God, and they're never disappointed. I believe you'll find that one of the common denominators among these believers is a cultivated approach to worship. They exalt the name of God at all times, they rejoice in the Lord always, and they see the power that is unleashed when they live that way.

Some of them are missionaries, fighting on the front lines of spiritual combat. I'd like to share such a story with you.

God's Power in Mombasa

The setting was Mombasa, a seaport city in southeastern Kenya. A missionary was holding a crusade with praise and worship as the focus. Kenya is a country with many believers—a place where God's Spirit is on the move. It's also a place where evil is very real and where demonic activity leaves its mark on the population. On this day, thousands of villagers had made long journeys from many points in East Africa to experience God's power in a mighty way.

It was half an hour before the service was to begin in the great gathering place, and large amplifiers were broadcasting worship and praise music. The lyrics were in English. Those in Nairobi, Mombasa, and the larger cities often speak English, but most of these provincial villagers couldn't understand the words they were hearing.

It really didn't seem to matter. The Spirit of God inhabited the praises, came victoriously through the great speakers, and instilled excitement in the hearts of the people. Many of them were hungry; many were travel-weary. And now they came to a place bathed in prayer and filled with heavenly, healthy music. Surely the Spirit of God was in this place, and the anticipation surged.

A new song began: "We are standing . . . on holy ground." An observer would later share that on that night, people spoke of hearing the demons scream when the first bars of that particular song passed through the speakers. This wasn't a writer's invention after the fact or some figurative language geared toward eloquence—it was the literal observation of many people who were there. I have missionaries in my own church who have told me that this often happens in the dark, Satan-dominated countries of the world. We here in the States know very little about this kind of demonic activity.

Right about here, I can feel some of you shifting uncomfortably in your seats. Once demons and angels enter the conversation, some of us raise an eyebrow. It challenges our conceptions of what is orthodox in our faith. We don't have many dealings with "spiritual hosts of wickedness in the heavenly places" (Ephesians 6:12). It's a different story on the mission field!

AN ALABAMA ADVENTURE

Our first line of defense in the naysaying of the supernatural is to confine it to Bible times. Our second is to concede that perhaps supernatural events happen far across the sea, in some exotic Third World setting we're never likely to behold. "These things may happen long ago and far away, but not in *my* neighborhood." That may not seem a like a good line of logic, but it has convinced millions of true believers.

That's why I'd like to share this story from the Heart of Dixie.

The year was 1987, and I remember following a disturbing series of articles in the newspaper. A rash of teenage suicides broke out in the southeastern corner of Alabama, and no one could quite provide an explanation. The tragedy of adolescent suicide is an ongoing social problem, but this was something different. Rick Hagens, a Southern Baptist preacher, sensed that some spiritual force was in play, some kind of demonic initiative with teenagers in the cross hairs. He knew that a satanic cult was nestled darkly in his community, and he sensed that the two phenomena were related.

Hagens spent a lot of time with young people, simply listening to their stories and their concerns. Many of them told him about devil worship and how it was a great preoccupation among their crowd. Everyone knew about the ring of devil worshipers, and it wasn't far out on the fringe; one of the most popular boys in the high school was involved. We'll call him Sheldon. Sheldon had seen enough of the satanic group and he wanted out. He quickly discovered, however, that this would be a matter much different than quitting the football team or running with a different crowd. He was warned that if he tried to leave the group, it would cost him his life.

Sheldon told his Christian friends about his plight so that, as he said, "If I'm found dead, you'll know who my murderers were." Perhaps it seemed like the expression of an overheated imagination. Teens are known to be melodramatic at times.

Tragically, Sheldon knew what he was talking about. A few weeks later, his lifeless body was pulled from a car. A hose from the exhaust pipe was taped to his wrist. In the eyes of the investigators and those who performed the autopsy, it had to be suicide—and that was the ruling. People thought it was tragic, and they marked it up to a terrible but unexplainable trend. But Rick Hagens's youth group knew better. Sheldon's classmates remembered his terrifying words, and they couldn't mark his death up to coincidence.

Rick knew this last death, foretold so pathetically by the victim, was a very loud wake-up call. He decided to mobilize the Christian community and focus on the issue of spiritual warfare. Rick talked to the right people at the police department and learned about the size and scope of the area's satanic cult. It wasn't just a matter of teenagers; adults were involved too. In at least one case, there was a minister known to belong to the circle. A detective told Rick that cult members were drawing names of other students whom they wanted to die. Targets would either be driven to take their own lives, or their murders would be arranged so as to resemble suicide.

Rick couldn't believe the things he was hearing. He told the police that he and every member of his task force were willing to help in any way possible. But this phenomenon went far beyond a matter of law enforcement or adolescent counseling; this was spiritual warfare at its deepest. Rick and his group members began going to all the key places in the community—the high schools and the areas known to be frequented by cult members—and they worshiped the Lord. They bathed the areas in prayers, praise, and hymns of God's greatness. They repeated this process every day for a week.

IN THE VALLEY OF THE SHADOW OF DEATH

One day Rick's team thought about the story of Elijah in the Old Testament. He, too, had been surrounded by evil in a land that should belong to God's people. Elijah had challenged the prophets of Baal to come to Mount Carmel and demonstrate the power of their god. The

God of Abraham, Isaac, and Jacob had won that contest in a rout, of course. God's power would always win such a confrontation.

So Rick decided to bring the crisis to a head. He got permission to speak on local radio and television, and there he issued a challenge to the devil worshipers. He dared them to meet him at their own favorite time and place: Halloween night in a graveyard. The enemy might have the home-field advantage, but he warned his opponents to take note: Jesus Christ would be attending with his group, and the victory had already been won, two thousand years ago.

It's easy to imagine that Rick and his friends were more than a little bit nervous. On Halloween night, when the stroke of midnight arrived, Rick was surrounded by his friends and supporters in the cemetery. He would later observe that he had always fought the devil with prayer and preaching, but tonight there was a different impression from God. The focus should be entirely on praise and worship. The group had come armed with a twelve-foot cross, and they planted it in the ground and lifted it high. There was also a bag of tracts to put in the hands of anyone interested. But the attention should not be on anything other than the exaltation of Christ. That's what the Holy Spirit's still, small voice seemed to be saying.

Rick's team gathered around the cross and began to sing. It was too dark for lyric sheets, so they sang from memory every chorus they could remember: "Just As I Am," "The Old Rugged Cross," many others. The believers praised God with all their hearts, and they felt empowered in their own unity and the comfort and assurance of the Holy Spirit.

Soon there was the rustle of dry grass, and dark shapes began to materialize in the midnight haze. The enemy was arriving. They had butchered a cow along the way and removed the entrails—a vicious act performed for no reason other than intimidation. Now, as their dark shapes emerged from the darkness, they formed a ring around Rick's huddled group, jeering and taunting. They had come in the costumes of evil spirits, vampires, and every other vestige of wickedness. Halloween, midnight, the cemetery, and now the images of demons themselves—not a sight we might ever have expected in the buckle of the Bible Belt.

No prayers of challenge were issued from the gritted teeth of Christians. There was no tough spiritual talk about strongholds or the binding of Satan. The believers simply ignored their would-be intimidators. Their business was to praise and worship the Lord, and it was a simple job description; they held to it. Rick's army drew strength from the Spirit of God and from the group's bond of unity as they circled the cross.

That's when the wonderful thing happened.

HOWLING INTO THE NIGHT

The power of praise began to move out from among Rick's group until it took firm hold of the crowd of devil worshipers. God's Spirit overwhelmed and undermined their evil. You could almost hear the air seeping out of them. The jeering and the taunting seemed to wither and fade; all trash-talking was silenced. The intimidators were intimidated. Satan's brigade now seemed astounded, transfixed; they hunkered down to the cold earth, where they sat silently listening to the sounds of worship for four hours. Not that there was anything artful from a musical perspective; Rick laughs about that idea. "We didn't even have a guitar," he said. This was just a group of Christians, huddled around a makeshift cross, singing the melodies of praise and worship.

It wasn't until four o'clock in the morning that the satanic cult members left—and they left quietly. All their brashness and arrogance had been stripped away. As it happened for Jehoshaphat, as it happened for Elijah, and as it happened in Mombasa, Kenya, the devil fled howling into the night, nursing his wounds. The record will show that this night marked the end of the teenage suicides. That trend was buried in the graveyard, under a wooden cross surrounded by worshipers.[1]

These examples of God's supernatural intervention are only as rare as we allow them to be. They're not reserved for "back then" or "over there." They're not stored away in heaven, pulled out only for high holy occasions. They're available to you and me through the overcoming power of God, whose might and wisdom is always available to keep the devil from winning even the smallest victory.

In the community where I live, there are devil worshipers. It's probably true wherever you may reside as well. We might choose to look the other way. We might choose to laugh them off as so many harmless crackpots following a fad. The devil would prefer that we look at it this way. He takes great pains to keep us reassured that he doesn't even exist. But in our world, Satan is alive and well. He takes hold of new territory every day, and he targets young people in particular. How do we meet that challenge? Legislation is no match for the evil one. Ignoring the trend won't help. Disbelieving is his delight.

Our only hope is to put on the full armor of God and take our stand. And the greatest weapon in our arsenal is worship. The wickedest maneuvers from the father of lies will never stand against the power of Christians uniting to praise and exalt God. It's wonderful to congregate in our sanctuaries for worship, but we need to take it to the streets. We need to be worshiping God every day, privately and with our families. We need to understand that worship isn't some formal, traditional ritual, but the most urgent business of serious Christians in an evil world.

Let me leave you with one practical way you can do that.

LET THE MUSIC PLAY

I feel a great debt of gratitude to songwriters and composers who have given us worship-based Christian music. These godly men and women of past and present generations have made it possible for us to express our heartfelt love and adoration to Almighty God.

Many hymns and worship songs have been written as vehicles of direct praise. By this, I mean these hymns are not songs *about* the Lord; they are worship songs *to* the Lord.

Several hymns are especially meaningful to me because they allow me to sing my love and adoration directly to the Lord. "Fairest Lord Jesus," "More Love to Thee, O Christ," "Great Is Thy Faithfulness," and "How Great Thou Art" are examples of direct-praise worship. And there are so many more recent hymns and choruses that reflect this same desire to come right into God's presence with singing.

"I Love You, Lord," "More Than Enough," "As the Deer Pants for the Water," "Jesus, I Just Want to Praise You," "Jesus, We Crown You with Praise," and "I Exalt You" are representative of the hundreds of newer songs that reflect direct praise. I sing these hymns and praise songs when I am driving, when I am walking, and often when I am in my study alone at night. The lyrics are generally lifted directly from Scripture, so how can I go wrong?

It is wonderful when a man tells his friends how much he loves his wife, but it is a far more intimate moment when he tells his wife how much he loves her. I love to sing *about* my love to the Lord, but I sense a deeper intimacy when I express that love directly *to* Him.

Perhaps this renaissance of worship and praise music has come about because of the times in which we live. There is so much noise pollution; the major secular labels often publish and promote "music" advocating crime, illicit sex, and disrespect for every authority. The cultural water we're drinking has been poisoned. Is it possible that the Holy Spirit is once again using the music of our faith to call us to a new standard of holy living and a deeper experience of fellowship with God?

I don't know what pressures your life may hold. Perhaps they come through job or school. Perhaps your source of anxiety is family turmoil. All of us have challenges that seem too great for us to contend with. It doesn't take being surrounded by a circle of devil worshipers in a graveyard; your own personal crises are spiritual warfare, too, when they threaten to overmaster you. How can you protect your mind and heart?

First, recognize the challenge for what it is. Any kind of problem is a spiritual issue. God wants to give you power and wisdom as you face it. Know that He has the answers to any question that may be dominating your life. Then commit yourself to give God the praise and the glory. Use music as a tool to help you praise God. Music has a way of taking hold of our emotions and expressing them in ways we cannot. Find some good praise music, either at a local Christian bookstore or by asking your friends at church to help you with recommendations.

Find a place of solitude, and then let the music guide you in lifting up the overcoming name of Christ. Use your Bible and the lyrics, and simply exalt and adore Him. I can assure you that if you'll do this time after time, your life will change in relation to your conflicts. Nothing will keep you down; no anxiety will overpower you. Like Paul and Silas in that prison, sing out from your cell and see if Almighty God doesn't begin to crumble those prison walls.

To truly worship God, of course, you'll need to come with clean hands and a clean heart. Don't expect this to be a quick fix if there is deep sin in your life—the Spirit of God will quickly bring that sin to your attention. But if your heart is pure and your life honors Him, praise and worship will give you victory over the worst that Satan can ever bring against you.

It's an interesting thing—where God is moving, unusual things seem to happen. It's always been that way, and it always will be. Supernatural events happen in Kenya and Alabama. Sure, but they can happen on the street where you live, too. Worship is the key that unlocks the door to wonderful things that God wants to accomplish in your life.

Consider this your call to worship. When was the last time you got away by yourself simply for the purpose of exalting Him for an extended period of time? When was the last time that you faced a great crisis, and your first impulse was to uplift the name of your Lord?

Believe me, resist the devil and he will flee from you. Praise the name of God and Satan's entire army will hit the highway. Wouldn't you like to see the devil's taillights and hear him screeching away, taking anxiety, pain, guilt, and fear with him?

It could happen to you—strange but true!

12

Worship in the Dark

TWELVE

A LOVELIER CHRISTIAN FAMILY you couldn't hope to find—a husband, his wife, and three wonderful children. Who would have guessed what lay ahead for them? And who could explain why?

It happened in the time when the family's cup of happiness was overflowing. Mom's prayers for another baby had been answered. The doctors told her a fourth child—a son—was on his way. Husband and wife were busily planning for the new arrival. And the best place for that kind of planning was the walks they took together.

Even before Mom's pregnancy, the couple had regularly enjoyed a "daily constitutional" just after dinner for exercise and chat. Now, with the baby coming, Mom felt the mild exercise made even more sense. But this evening, on their way out the door, the phone rang. It was an important business call Dad had been expecting. "Go on ahead," he whispered to his wife, his hand over the transmitter. "I'll come jogging to catch up with you in a minute."

But the phone call lasted just a bit longer than he had expected. Just a few extra minutes—tragic extra minutes.

In the same little neighborhood, a teenager pulled the family car into his driveway. As he emerged, he saw the scrape on the fender. The sight confirmed his worst suspicions.

During his drive, the young man had heard and felt an unsettling *thump*. He hadn't seen a thing, but it felt as if the car had hit a dog, a deer, or something of the kind. That's what he told his father a few moments later. Father didn't like the sound of it. He said, "Let's get in the car and retrace your route. We need to know what it was that scraped the fender."

And so they backed out of the driveway and retraveled the young man's original route. As they cruised slowly along, they came across a neighbor who also seemed to be looking for something. Father rolled down the window and asked what it might be. "I'm looking for my wife," said the neighbor. "We were heading out for a walk, but she left before me while I was on the phone. Now I can't seem to find her."

Yes, the next portion of this story is obvious enough. After another moment, both parties had found what they were looking for. Her neck was broken, and she was lying in a ditch—dead. A lovely Christian mother carried into the next world the child who never saw the light of day. Two separate families were torn with grief.

Why would such a thing happen in this world? Why would it happen to good people? How could God, loving and merciful, allow such a thing?

When I first heard this story, I shook my head sadly. And yet it's just one of countless such stories you and I hear in a lifetime—every year, really. I imagine you could share a tale just as true and just as tragic. Most of us know the feeling of personal catastrophe far too intimately.

148

The story in itself isn't so hard to believe; what I find more amazing is the sequel.

In a small Baptist church in that very community, a few weeks later, a man stood up to address the congregation one Sunday. The whole church fell silent as they watched him rise, slowly and sadly, yet purposely. He cleared his throat and began to speak of the goodness of God. He praised the name of the sovereign Lord who rules every part of this world and every part of our lives. Before his amazed friends and acquaintances, he testified to the *goodness* and *grace* of God in times of suffering and loss. To God be the glory—always, in hard times and good ones.

Life has its holocausts—that's not news. The real story is the persistence of glory rising from the ashes. How is it that within the context of the worst life can dish out, many people come to love and to glorify God more deeply?

Deeper Even Than Doubt

I don't know the whys and the wherefores of the evil that is allowed to afflict us. It's an enigma whose answers won't be unraveled in this lifetime. But the worst of misery is overshadowed by the wonder of faith; we marvel when people can look into the sky after it has fallen upon them with a crash and whisper, "Praise the Lord *anyway!*"

Do you remember the story of Job? In the midst of his prosperity came unthinkable tragedy. He lost his livelihood, his servants, and finally his children. In a matter of hours, nearly all that he had, all that he had labored for, had been swept away. Here is how he responded:

> Then Job arose, tore his robe, and shaved his head; and he fell to the ground and worshiped. And he said:

149

"Naked I came from my mother's womb,
And naked shall I return there.
The LORD gave, and the LORD has taken away;
Blessed be the name of the LORD."

—JOB 1:20–21

But that's just a Bible character from ancient times, right? No—Job was a historical human being who faced trials as people in all times face trials. But we also know that people in all times, and not Job alone, have faced them in the power and strength of worship. Like Job, they have expressed, not denied, their grief. They have slumped to the ground in tears and then moved to their knees in worship. An everyday worship mind-set allows us to see life's highs and lows through the same lens that Job looked through. It helps us to see that we came naked into this world, and we are entitled to nothing by right. "Whereas you do not know what will happen tomorrow. For what is your life? It is even a vapor that appears for a little time and then vanishes away" (James 4:14).

That's only the starting point. We are dust on our way to ashes, yet the Lord Himself counts us worthy of His love. We face every kind of trial, but Almighty God comes to comfort us. And we as Christians know that death hasn't written the final chapter. So at the very bottom of the deepest pit, we feel our grief and our anger. We shake our fists at heaven for a moment, and afterward heaven is still there. God is still all-powerful, and He will give us the power to prevail. We can see this only when we live each day in the spirit of worship. It allows us to come through the storm and say, "Blessed be the name of the Lord!"

The prophet Habakkuk, of course, was a fist shaker. He was one of those who dared to question God, a minor prophet with major questions. He carried on a dialogue with the Creator that constitutes his entire book in the Old Testament. It's a great pity that his conversation with God lies in one of those neglected neighborhoods of the Scriptures. We should travel there more often.

One of the most intriguing elements of this book is that it seems to have musical origins. Habakkuk 3:19 tells us it was written for the "chief musician," and the only other place where we find the musical annotation "selah" is the Psalms. So what we have here seems to be a kind of duet between God and His questioning child, as recorded for the people's use. In its opening overture, at least, it is the music of misery. Yet it is also the source of a certain joy, for this book is the ultimate source text of the Protestant Reformation. It is in Habakkuk 2:4b where we read, "The just shall live by his faith," the battle cry of the movement started by Martin Luther and John Calvin that rediscovered the priesthood of every believer.

Sorry I Asked!

The name *Habakkuk* literally means "the one who embraces." What a wonderful image, for here is a man who comes to God with all his unanswered questions. He finally comprehends that the answers will have to wait—at least for the duration of this earthly life. But for now, there is the loving embrace of God. And finally we discover that embrace is sufficient for us, just as it was for Habakkuk. If the overture is remorseful, the finale is an anthem of victory, an ode to joy.

Habakkuk looks upon his world and asks, "Why is it that the wicked seem to prosper? Why do the wrong people seem to get all the rewards and good soldiers get raw deals?"

We, too, see too much evil—pornography, drugs, violence, crime, and outright rebellion toward God and His laws. We look upward and ask, "Lord? Aren't You going to do something about this?"

Habakkuk has those questions, and his response is to pray. But after awhile it seems to him that God has no interest in his prayers. "How long do I have to pray?" Habakkuk asks in frustration. "Have You heard a word I've said? I've brought before You the wickedness of this land; why don't You do something?"

Finally God answers Habakkuk's concerns, but Habakkuk won't exactly be satisfied with what he hears. It seems that just as he finds the answers, someone has changed the questions!

It starts out promising indeed. God tells Habakkuk to be patient, because God is about to do something incredible. "Be utterly astounded!" He says (Habakkuk 1:5). He also says, in a loose paraphrase, "If I tried to tell you, you wouldn't believe Me. But the wicked will get theirs."

So far, so good. But then comes the part that must have made Habakkuk choke. God drops this bomb: "I am raising up the Chaldeans" (Habakkuk 1:6).

The *Chaldeans?* Are You serious, Lord?

The Chaldeans, who came from the southern portion of Babylon, were the wickedest people on the map. God once sent Jonah to see them in Nineveh, and Jonah took off in the other direction. There was a reason any right-thinking prophet would want no part of that nation. As Jonah later said to God, it was unthinkable even to *consider* the Chaldeans escaping judgment. These were people who slew infants and offered them to idols. These were people who butchered their enemies in battle, far beyond the customs of warfare in that day. They seemed to have no conscience, no remorse, and no reluctance to overrun any nation in their sights. Indeed, the fear was that the Chaldeans would engulf the known world with their military power and their savagery.

But God hasn't forgotten any of this. As a matter of fact, He immediately catalogs all the atrocities and outrages of the Chaldeans. But He's going to be using them just the same.

Habakkuk is shaking his head, trying to take all this in. He asks:

> Are You not from everlasting,
> O LORD my God, my Holy One?
> We shall not die.
> O LORD, You have appointed them for judgment;
> O Rock, You have marked them for correction.
>
> —HABAKKUK 1:12

And there we have what we might call the overture to this philosophical opera. The rest of the score is a divine duet between God and Habakkuk, dealing with the questions that have been raised. And we recognize the melody well. Most of us have found ourselves singing this song—different verse, same as the first.

TAKING THE HIGH ROAD

One of the things I really enjoy is speaking at Bible conferences. For one thing, I love teaching the Bible. But I must also admit that I love teaching the Bible in a beautiful retreat setting. There are camps placed in the middle of beautiful mountain greenery—where God paints the scenery, as the old Rodgers and Hart song puts it. On a visit there, I can get out and tramp around in the woods, a sheer delight. I can enjoy the breeze, feel the leaves crackle beneath my shoes, and enjoy the beautiful artwork of heaven.

On such hikes I find that it's not unusual to come to a wet, mucky place where movement becomes treacherous. Experienced backpackers know all about these situations. The first thing to do is to look for a little plot of ground above the waterline, a place that remains dry and comfortable. A little bit of careful observation will show you that these dry spots make a certain pattern, and the skillful hiker can move from one to the other without sinking into the muck.

That's what Habakkuk is doing. He's looking for the safe and comforting pattern that might help him navigate his way through the swamp of problems. In verses 12 and 13, he hits many of the "high spots" of his Creator:

He is eternal.
"Are You not from everlasting?"

He is holy.
"O LORD my God, my holy One."

He is sovereign.
"You have appointed them for judgment."

He is mighty.
"You have marked them for correction."

He is pure.
"You are of purer eyes than to behold evil."

Habakkuk's journey as a prophet had grown treacherous. Around him, all other ground was sinking sand. But these five places, he knew, were secure. We can take our stand on these firm foundations. We can keep moving when nothing around us seems to be dependable. How many times have I done the same? Too many to count, and I hope you've done likewise.

As we are faced with some terrible crisis, some awful calamity, we stop to review the lowest common denominators of faith. Death is staring us in the face—*but He is eternal.* We're surrounded by so much that is wicked—*but He is holy.* The rats keep winning the rat race—*but He appoints them for judgment.* When it seems as if the whole world is sinking into the muck, we need not remain in the valley. We can set hind's feet on high places, like the deer. We can lift up our eyes, and our spirits and confidence will follow. Habakkuk's name means "the one who embraces," but it also means "the one who clings." We can cling to God for dear life, and we can do it by setting foot on each of these principles.

First Steps

It's true of each part of your life. In your marriage, your family, your work, and your health, for example, you can think back and remember the high spots as well as the swampy grounds. I can remember some of those low places very well. I've awakened with the immediate, grim realization of some crisis I was weathering at the time. It's terrible to start the day with a dark thought, but it happens to all of us. In those times, I've swung my feet out of bed to the soft carpet, and I've consciously directed my thoughts in this direction:

Lord, I'm so anxious today; I'm so afraid of stumbling. But I choose to set my feet on the firm ground as You guide me. Only You will lead me in pleasant pastures and beside still waters. Only You can restore my soul. You know the deep, unsettled emotions I'm feeling. You know that I'm walking through the Valley of the Shadow right now, but You will always be with me. I choose to take my stand upon Your holiness. I choose to take my stand upon Your goodness, Your faithfulness, Your sovereignty. It's a dark and a low valley, but You will lead me on to safety. Today I will use Your Word as a lamp unto my feet and a light unto my path. That light will direct me to the high places, and I will not give in to the sinking sand that surrounds me.

Let me leave you with some first steps that will take you from the murk and the misery to the high and dry. When you discover yourself sunk deep into doubt, and God no longer seems real to you, make it a point to take these steps from worry to worship:

1. *Admit* to yourself the doubt into which you've fallen. Don't deny your emotions and try toughing it out on your own. You'll only sink deeper and deeper into the quicksand. Instead, say what's really on your mind—right out loud. Go to a place of solitude and admit your doubts. Admit your frustration with God. Take a careful inventory of the things in life that have your stomach tied in knots. You won't be counting your blessings as much as your "distressings." It's not a destination, but it's a start!

2. *Acknowledge* to God what you've just told yourself. Don't worry, He's big enough to take it; He knows what you're feeling, anyway. Just clear the air between your Lord and you.

3. *Attribute* to God His various traits. Take the passage we've just studied, or some other passage from Scripture that lists His attributes. You'll find so many of them in the psalms. Try Psalm 8. List these characteristics of our Lord and meditate upon them, one by one. What does it mean that He is holy? Bring a dictionary and look up each of these terms—it will broaden your perspective as you go over these words. How is He sovereign? What are the implications of His eternal nature?

4. *Apply* these attributes to your unique situation. If God is holy,

how does that affect you? If He is eternal, what does that say about your problem? If He is sovereign, how should you be feeling about things? Take all the uncertainty, all the anxiety, all the specifics of your current state and lay them right up alongside the perfection of God. This is a big step. It brings you near to cleansing worship.

5. *Add* the ultimate attribute. God is love. Read 1 John 4:16–18a and take a giant step onto that high place in the Word of God. Cling to it: "And we have known and believed the love that God has for us. God is love, and he who abides in love abides in God, and God in him. Love has been perfected among us in this: that we may have boldness in the day of judgment; because as He is, so are we in this world. There is no fear in love; but perfect love casts out fear." If you take time right now to memorize that verse, implanting it in your heart, you'll be girding yourself for countless low valleys that lie in your future.

6. *Abide* in God's love, just as John has urged us. Imagine the love of God expressed in His great arms enfolding you and protecting you. He is love, and He casts out your fear. Let the tears flow if they come. Let them wash away the impurities that drove you away from His loving arms.

7. *Adore* Him. Sing your favorite songs of praise. Read your favorite Bible passages about worship. Tell God about your love for Him, and express your gratitude for all that He is doing for you.

These are the trenches of worship in everyday experience. If you take these seven steps with sincerity and determination, I guarantee you that you'll find yourself in the transforming presence of God. And I guarantee that you'll come away as a new person with new perspective and new strength. You'll be looking at life from the high places, and you'll be breathing the clearest and most delicious air there is. You'll be looking almost into the reaches of eternity itself, and no problem in the world will be able to master you as it's done before.

I hope you won't think of Habakkuk as the prophet with the fancy vocabulary. Those words he gave us are words of power. They connect us to the truth of God that is so easily forgotten, and they give us something to take hold of when we're sinking fast. Cling to God's holiness. Establish your footing on God's sovereignty, and wrap your arms around His purity.

> My hope is built on nothing less,
> Than Jesus' blood and righteousness;
> I dare not trust the sweetest frame,
> But wholly lean on Jesus' name.
>
> When darkness seems to hide His face
> I rest on His unchanging grace;
> In ev'ry high and stormy gale,
> My anchor holds within the veil.
>
> His oath, His covenant, His blood
> Support me in the whelming flood;
> When all around my soul gives way,
> He then is all my hope and stay.
>
> On Christ, the solid Rock, I stand;
> All other ground is sinking sand,
> All other ground is sinking sand.[1]

13

Knowledge and Trust

Thirteen

Knowledge and Trust

BRUCE LARSON TELLS THE STORY of a pleasant visit to the Gulf of Mexico. At least it began pleasantly enough. Danger never sends advance notice—it springs upon us unawares.

Larson had a small boat, and he suddenly spotted it drifting away. Somehow he hadn't secured the little vessel, and it was being pulled away by the tide. Impulsively, Larson leapt into the water and swam out to retrieve his property.

He hadn't realized just how far away the boat had drifted—or how far away from the shore he had already moved in his determined pursuit. It dawned on him that the distance from safety greatly exceeded the remaining strength in his body. He no longer had what it took to swim back to shore. *Well, this is the end,* he thought, as the waves lashed him up and down again. *I have nothing left; I'm done for.* Those waves were certainly high ones, and the sky was dark.

That's when the voice of God brought a word of salvation.

I'm here, Larson, he fancied the voice saying, *and you're not coming home as soon as you think. Can you tread water?*

Larson had thought in terms of swimming, not treading. He would have spent all his energy and then gone down like a rock if he'd tried to swim. Instead, he relaxed and continued to tread water as the waves pushed him back in to safety.[1]

Larson's story reminds me a bit of that little children's toy, the Chinese finger trap. It's a colorful little tube of flax, and you place a finger in each end. The child laughs in delight when his fingers won't pull out. The more he pulls, the tighter becomes the grip of the trap. After a moment, he figures it out; it's simply a matter of relaxing his fingers and letting them slip out easily.

Maybe you're an assertive person like me, and perhaps your tendency is to lash out frantically in every direction when you find yourself in a bad spot. Quite often the real danger is our strenuous exertions to make things right. Like Larson, we make the mistake of relying on our own strength. Deliverance comes in the quiet attitude of listening to what God says. More often than not, if we'll relax and trust, we'll find ourselves drifting to safety.

But do we really trust? That's the $64,000 question—and the issue we'll take up in this chapter.

Habakkuk, as we learned in the preceding pages, had a first reaction much like Larson's. He lashed out. He thought in terms of human strength and logic: *How can you allow this, God? Our nation is dangerously adrift! And how can you use the Chaldeans, of all people?*

To which the voice of God essentially replied, *I'm still here, Habakkuk. Relax. Tread water for a few minutes, and watch the wonderful things I will do.*

FROM WHY TO WONDER TO WORSHIP

Habakkuk's book shows how he traveled the road from why to wonder—then, finally, to worship. Each of us encounters pain and tragedy. In a time of terrible loss, we wonder how we can even go on living.

And yet we see wise people who are capable of worshiping through the tears of mourning. The pain is real, but that pain is undergirded by a powerful faith that God is good and that everything has a meaning. How do we handle the holocaust of September 11, 2001? As far as I know, there are no fewer Christians than before that date. On the contrary, I believe many individuals came to faith, or to a revival of faith, through the terrible national attack and tragedy. Our faith isn't shaken by catastrophe; it's only strengthened, for we turn with new yearning and new dependence to the One who embraces us. And we find His arms strong enough to hold us, just as He has held His hurting children for so many thousands of years. History brings perspective, but we have to let Him hold us. We have to trust.

As God began speaking to Habakkuk, the change in the prophet was dramatic. He began to see with new eyes. Listen to the close of his book:

> Though the fig tree may not blossom,
> Nor fruit be on the vines;
> Though the labor of the olive may fail,
> And the fields yield no food;
> Though the flock may be cut off from the fold,
> And there be no herd in the stalls—
> Yet I will rejoice in the LORD,
> I will joy in the God of my salvation.

My Heart's Desire

The Lord God is my strength;
He will make my feet like deer's feet,
And He will make me walk on my high hills.

—HABAKKUK 3:17–19

Aren't those words magnificent? This is absolutely one of my favorite passages in all the Word of God. The prophet is saying, "Our crops may fail. Our flocks may wander. No matter what happens, I will praise God. And the day will come when He will take me to the highest peaks of joy."

This is the ultimate expression of faith and worship. Habakkuk recognizes that times may be good, times may be bad, and circumstances may waver—but none of it has anything to do with our praise and worship. Our adoration remains constant because He remains constant. This is how Job can lose his family, his friends, his home, and his every possession, yet love God all the more deeply. This is how a man can see his wife violently taken from him, body broken in a ditch with their unborn child, and rise to proclaim that God is no less faithful, no less loving.

This is why those who don't know God are consumed by the fires of life, yet those who trust God are refined by those same fires. It's the power of knowledge and trust.

The Secret of Inner Strength

We all know that people and their faith are like trees in the forest. Some are uprooted when the first harsh wind comes along; others draw on a deep strength from the very foundation, and they continue to stand firm. Their roots only dig deeper; their bark only grows thicker.

What is it that makes the difference? How can some people keep praising God even when life becomes harsh and cruel? It's one of the great secrets of life, but we can find the clues in these three short chapters of Habakkuk, taking a man from tragedy to triumph, from worry to worship, from preoccupation to praise.

Here is the greatest clue of all, so attend closely: *We worship whom we trust, and we trust whom we know.*

Halt! Don't read on too quickly; take a moment to let that statement sink in. The depths of its wisdom are deceptive.

Worship is only validated through its constancy. Everyone who ever attended a church camp as a teenager and had the proverbial "mountaintop experience" can tell you how easy it is to worship at high emotional altitudes. For a few days they have great fun with their friends. They hear powerful preaching. They dig into their Bibles, and—often for the first time—they focus on the reality of God with a laserlike intensity. The result is rapture! It's the first bloom of the love of God through worship. At the end, of course, a counselor stands by the campfire and delivers the dreaded "down in the valley" speech. You remember that one, don't you? "Kids, it's easy to worship God up here on the mountaintop. But tomorrow, you'll go back to your families, back to your unchurched friends. It's a lot harder to hang onto your faith down in the valley."

Of course that counselor is wise. But there needs to come a time in life, farther down the road, when our faith sinks beneath skin level— when it seeps down to the soul so that, even in the worst of times, even down in the valley, we praise and worship God. Praise isn't the response to favorable circumstances; it's the element that runs even deeper, setting the tone of our approach to those circumstances.

And how do we reach that level of faith? Listen again: *We worship whom we trust, and we trust whom we know.* We come to this level of faith because we build trust, and we build trust because we spend time with God. Do you remember the experience of getting to know your best friend—perhaps the person you married? At first, there were "probationary" occasions. You didn't fully unburden your deepest thoughts because you didn't know whether you could trust your new friend. Alas, there are lesser relationships with people who fall by the wayside because they betray our trust in some way. But your best friend was that person who redeemed your trust, and you confirmed it only through the time and tears of relationship.

The same principle holds true with God. You must come to know Him before you can really, truly, deeply trust Him. Then and only then will you be able to worship in spirit and in truth. Then and only then will you be able to say, in a twenty-first-century paraphrase of Habakkuk, "I may lose my work, my loved ones, and all that I own. Still I will love God all the more. Still I will praise Him with the loudest voice I can muster. And He will lift me up, for I know whom I have believed and am persuaded that He is able."

It's Not What You Know, but Whom You Know

We come to an urgent issue for today's Christians. Those who attend my church often tell me they're attracted by our emphasis on God's Word—and rightly so. "You don't preach your opinion or your spin or your flavor of faith," they say. "We get into God's Word and we see exactly what He has to say." Our members affirm that they learn a great deal about the Bible simply by attending our worship services.

That's a good thing. But it's not good enough.

It's possible to focus so intensely on gaining knowledge *about* God that we miss the knowledge *of* God. The difference there is one of eternal, infinite magnitude. It's the difference between seeing an old, faded picture of a distant relative and sitting in your granddaddy's lap.

It's the difference between reading a scientific, statistical report about the vitamins in beef and biting into a thick sirloin steak hot off the grill. It's the difference between knowing facts about God and experiencing His powerful presence.

I believe that as a whole, we modern evangelical Christians are far guiltier of dry intellectual faith than we ever want to realize. Ultimately it feels so much safer to limit ourselves to sharing information about the Lord. As human creatures, we feel drawn to Him from the day we're born, even before we realize it. We yearn to fill the void that lies in the center of our hearts and souls. We make a long journey to His throne room, and just outside the doorway—we stop. We're like the Cowardly Lion who had to be dragged into the great room where the Wizard of Oz held court. *What will God say? How will He interfere with my life?* Deep inside, we're afraid to approach that throne, to stand within His reach. And here we come back around to the issue of *trust.*

To trust God, we must know Him. But to come to know God, we must first trust Him, at least a little bit—right? Some of us spend the entire duration of our spiritual lives going around in that circle.

Do you remember learning to ride a bicycle? It was a trust issue— nothing more, nothing less. There came a time when you had to take the training wheels off, place your feet on the pedals, and allow that bike to take flight down the street. Admit it—you were terrified! Perhaps Mom or Dad attempted every maneuver and spoke every word they could think of in a desperate attempt to reassure you. But you had to trust that bike. You had to realize that even if you fell—once, even twice—you were going to end up on an exhilarating ride, with the trees rushing by and the wind blowing your hair. It would be worth the learning curve.

You wanted to know bike riding, but you first had to trust the bicycle itself. No textbook, no parental word of advice would accomplish the mission. But once you did it—once you made the leap of faith—you never again lost the aptitude for bike riding. Why? *Trust.*

My church, like most, is filled with wonderful people, many of whom know the Lord intimately. They've taken that wonderful ride, and they've felt the exhilarating wind of the Holy Spirit blowing through their lives. But I'm certain that there are many others who are afraid to take off their spiritual training wheels. Training wheels allow us to make a pretense of bike riding, but we know it's not remotely the same thing as really riding the bike.

To experience the fullness of worship, we must trust the One we worship. And to trust Him, we must know Him. Do you see the significance here? Have you ever felt as if you knew all the facts about God, but your prayers never passed the ceiling? Have you ever sung a hymn without being able to bring the words to life? Have you ever realized that your morning devotions have become a dry Bible study rather than a warm visit with your heavenly Father? You wanted to worship in spirit and in truth; you felt good about the latter, but not the former.

We need truth, and we need sound theology. The right information is essential. But above all else, we need *relationship*. Once we've come into His powerful and loving presence, we'll never struggle to trust Him again—any more than we'll have to take a refresher course in bike riding.

Reading between the Lines

I heard about a young lady who loved to read. One day a friend brought her a book with the highest recommendations. "This one's a must-read," said the friend. "You need to read it this week."

So the young lady read the book—laboriously, as it turned out. It was her habit never to replace a volume on the shelves without completing it, even if she had to struggle to make it through. And that's just what she did. This was the most boring book she'd ever held in her hands. It was a joy to get back to her usual fare.

The next week, her friend dropped by to take her to a party. The young lady was hoping the subject of the book wouldn't arise, because then she'd have to state her honest opinion. But the friend never mentioned it. And the young lady's thoughts were soon elsewhere, because she found the host of the party fascinating. As a matter of fact, she fell in love with him during the next few weeks. All aglow, she told her friend what was happening. Her friend laughed aloud. "I knew you'd like that book," she said. "But I didn't think you'd take it to this extreme!"

Surprised, the young lady asked, "What in the world are you talking about?"

"Oh, my—did I forget to tell you why I brought that book to you?" she asked. "It was to help you make conversation at the party. The author is none other than your new love interest!"

I needn't tell you the young lady scrambled back to the shelf and grabbed that volume for the second time, with renewed interest. In the course of that evening she took in every word once again. It was the greatest book she'd ever read, by far. She reread it eight times and bought copies for everyone she knew. And her own copy is lovingly inscribed by the author.

It makes a great deal of difference to know someone rather than simply to know their words. By this time in my life I possess a great deal of information about the Scriptures, and I revere every inspired word of that book. I can't imagine a day without turning its pages. But if I didn't know the Author, how cold those ancient chapters would be. Why would I care about reading Nahum—or Habakkuk, for that matter?

Why would I keep reading the Gospels, and Paul's letters, for the three hundredth time?

The difference, you see, is that I've met and fallen in love with the One who gave us those writings, and it makes all the difference. His loving inscription is in my heart.

Get the Picture?

Not long ago I was reading about the life of Count Von Zinzendorf, the key man in the birth of the modern Moravian church. He had one of the greatest missionary hearts of any Christian who ever lived, and he sent out spiritual pioneers to early America and elsewhere. This was long before most modern mission services were even born. Von Zinzendorf was a pious man, and his emphasis never veered away from his direct and personal knowledge of the person of Christ.

One day the Count visited a museum of fine art. He walked through the doors in the early afternoon, and he was still there five hours later. But he hadn't taken in all the paintings and exhibits. He had remained all that time in one spot, without ever moving to the right or the left. The curator began to be concerned. It was time to close the building, and this quiet man was rooted to that spot as if he were one of the exhibits himself, perhaps a finely sculpted statue—except that he was seated on the floor, staring up at a picture.

The curator followed his gaze and saw a fine canvas inspired by the Book of Revelation. The subject was the holy Lamb of God. Count Von Zinzendorf must have had every tiny detail memorized by now. The curator walked over behind him, gently placed a hand on the man's shoulder, and started to speak. But now he saw something he hadn't previously noticed—tears rolling down Von Zinzendorf's cheeks.

Underneath the painting was this inscription: "If He cared that much for you, what should your concern be for Him?"

It was clear that Von Zinzendorf had given five hours to the contemplation of that question. He was lost in the greatness and the love of Christ, who had given His all for him. Unaware of the time, even forgetful perhaps of where he was, the Count was worshiping deeply, profoundly, and emotionally.[2]

I would like to see that painting. But perhaps it wouldn't strike you or me with the same impact. It's entirely possible that it wasn't even a particularly notable work of art. I believe the painting so profoundly moved Count Von Zinzendorf because the subject of the canvas was already the dearest to him, his Lord, his Master, his great love, and his closest friend. The Count knew how to connect with God and to praise Him wherever he might be, even in an art museum. You and I might have had our "art appreciation" hats on, and it wouldn't have occurred to us to worship God, even when we came across a canvas with spiritual content. But your "worship hat" should always be on your head. A beautiful sky, a friend's smile, or a completed task is all the reason you should need to take a moment in your day for the wonder of worship.

That may be a struggle right now. But the day you stand before Him and look deeply into His eyes, all your distrust and all your ambivalence will melt away. Your only concern will be the wish for a thousand tongues to sing His praise. You'll know the very depths of worship in truth—but yes, in spirit, too.

14

At the Door of Eternity

FOURTEEN

At the Door of Eternity

AND SO, deep into our exploration together, we find ourselves back at the place where we began—on the threshold of the great throne room of God. You may want to reread the first chapter in which we took that first step into the presence of the King of kings. We stood with John, the beloved disciple, in the setting he described in Revelation 4. Awestruck, we stepped into that great chamber of light where the angels attend the King who is above all kings and praise the Name that is above every name.

It takes only a simple reading of Revelation 4:1–11 to feel chills of excitement making their way up our spines. Imagine being there! At the end of the previous chapter (and remember, biblical chapter divisions were added late in the game, hundreds of years later), Jesus has said to one of the seven churches, "Behold, I stand at the door and knock" (Revelation 3:20a). And He has issued an invitation: Simply open the door, invite Him in, and He will come in and dine. It's a cozy, intimate image of our fellowship with the Savior.

But now, in Revelation 4, the tables are turned. It is we who stand at His door. It is we who step into His home. Daniel Baumann said, "Worship is a stairway on which there is movement in two directions: God comes to man, and man goes to God."[1] In Revelation, it's not a stairway, but a doorway.

John describes that door standing open, a portal that communicates between heaven and earth. Then he hears a voice "like a trumpet," saying, "Come up here, and I will show you things which must take place after this" (Revelation 4:1c). Immediately, John tells us, he is in the Spirit; and he beholds the throne and the King who sits upon it. Surely such a scene is beyond description, but the throne is bathed in a rainbow's radiance, John says. It gleams like an emerald.

Only when he has taken this in, only when he has surely fallen to his knees and begun weeping, does John notice the other, lesser thrones—twenty-four of them. Great men are seated here, adorned in blinding white robes. Crowns of gold shine from their hair. In any worldly setting, they themselves might seem worthy of praise; here, one almost misses the elegant elders in the presence of their King.

Lightning flashes from the throne. Thunder roars all around it, and there are celestial voices. These are the sounds of a heavenly storm, a storm of impending judgment. And there are many things that we, with John, struggle to understand. "Seven lamps of fire were burning before the throne," he observes, "which are the seven Spirits of God" (v. 5b). There is a glittering sea of glass, of crystal, before the throne, and then there are the creatures—surely the strangest apparitions beheld by John's eyes. One is like a lion, one resembles a calf, one is manlike, and the fourth seems to be a great eagle. But all of them have many eyes "around and within"; and all have six wings. These creatures are given totally to worship, for all eternity, and they sing:

Holy, holy, holy,

Lord God Almighty,

Who was and is and is to come! (v. 8b)

The four living creatures give glory, honor, and praise to the King of kings, over and over. And as they do so, the twenty-four elders, in the form and fashion of kings, follow their lead. They fall on their faces before the throne, casting down their golden crowns upon that glassy sea. Do you recognize the scene laid out in the hymn, "Holy, Holy, Holy"? The song of the elders goes like this:

You are worthy, O Lord,

To receive glory and honor and power;

For You created all things,

And by Your will they exist and were created. (v. 11)

So we stand with John, and we take it all in, or we at least make the attempt. Perhaps it takes us all in. For the question is, How would we emerge from witnessing such a sight? What would happen if you and I truly stood for but a moment in the throne room of eternity? The invitation is open. Jesus stands at our door, knocking and hoping to enter our humble dwelling. Then His own door is left ajar, inviting us to step out of this temporal, fallen world for a moment and behold the true, uncovered majesty that lies at the center of the cosmos: the gleaming rainbow radiance, the roaring lightning and thunder, the shimmering sea of crystal before the throne, all the kings and creatures of creation expending themselves in abject worship.

How would you be changed?

AN AUDIENCE WITH THE KING

Wheaton College in Illinois once had a gracious, godly chancellor named V. Raymond Edman. He was a missionary, a college president, an educator, an author, and a friend to countless Christians and seekers alike. Billy Graham once called him the most unforgettable Christian he ever met. Something of a quiet legend in his own time among evangelicals, Dr. Edman wrote a number of books cherished by those who knew his love and devotion to Christ. The chancellor died in 1967 in the most appropriate setting imaginable—though surely traumatic to those who were there. He passed on while preaching the chapel service at Wheaton. And his topic was worship.

That morning, Dr. Edman shared with his listeners a personal anecdote. It involved his meeting with the king of Ethiopia some years earlier. In order to have an audience with the king, he had to observe strict protocol. If he didn't meet and follow through on each criterion, he wouldn't be judged worthy of coming into this king's presence. Dr. Edman then drew a parallel with attending weekday chapel services at Wheaton. "You have an audience with the King of kings," he said. The ruler of Ethiopia or any other nation would fall on his face and cast his crown in the presence of the Almighty.

Dr. Edman wondered if those in the audience really comprehended the awesome act of worship. He went on to offer practical suggestions of how to make chapel more meaningful, how to come to a better realization of being in the transforming presence of God. And just like that, in the very midst of his wise and godly counsel, Edman himself was taken from among them. He had gone on to meet the Lord face to face. It was the last and greatest sermon illustration V. Raymond Edman ever shared.

At the time, this event was well publicized. Many Christian journalists and leaders reflected upon it, and many of them offered virtually the same words. Their observation was that surely Dr. Edman had as seamless a transition into God's presence as any man or woman could wish. His very life was spent in worship as an ultimate lifestyle: worship through missions and evangelism, worship through friendship, worship through teaching, worship through constant praise and adoration of his Maker. Dr. Edman's love for God was first and foremost, though he had no shortage of love to offer those around him. He seemed to be in the very presence of God just moments before he died, and he went to experience that presence at the final and greatest level. Everything in his life had led logically and consistently to that moment when his joy would finally be made full.[2]

In traditional worship, we often have three emphases: praising, praying, and preaching. When the world passes away, and we come into God's presence for all eternity, only one of those three great pillars of worship will still stand: *praise.*

Preaching? We'll have no further need for it, as we'll all understand fully. I suppose I'll be looking for another job, for there will be no place for sermons in heaven.

Prayer? We won't need to confess; we won't need supplication. And in terms of communicating with God, why speak by telephone when you're in the very presence of the other party?

Yet one portion of prayer, of course, is praise and adoration. It will continue on infinitely, into the depths of eternity itself.

A BOOK OF DOORS

I would like to be more like V. Raymond Edman. I'd like my life to be a consistent line of praise and worship that leads to its logical culmination, so that my transition into God's presence will be a seamless one. If the business of praise carries on from here to eternity, then it's serious business indeed. And I need to know more about how to worship and to praise my Father, for it's the essential task that connects my temporal life with my eternal one.

Perhaps praise is the doorway to that next world. For John in the fourth chapter of his Revelation, it all began with a doorway that opened from this world into the next. On this side, the isle of Patmos; on the other, the aisles of Paradise. His eyes must have been wide; his heart must have pounded fiercely. How could he behold such a thing and live? And yet the greatest miracle of all is that we can stand there beside him. Through the lovely poetry that the Holy Spirit brought us from his hand, we can see all that John saw. We can peer through that doorway into eternity.

John might be called the Doorkeeper of the New Testament. In the letter to the church at Philadelphia, John has mentioned an open door set before those people—a door of opportunity. In his letter to the Laodicean church, as we've mentioned, Jesus had stood at the door and knocked. And in Revelation 19, there will be still another door. Jesus will come charging through it on a white stallion to conquer His enemies and begin establishing His kingdom on earth. Revelation is all about portals by which Christ crosses our threshold and we cross His— a revolving door between heaven and earth.

Through the incredible doorway described in Revelation 4, John witnesses the ultimate passion and pageantry of worship. The imagery is so rich that we struggle to keep it all in our heads. The ideas are so profound that we struggle to face the implications of our lives and how they will change in the aftermath.

We've taken note of the crystal sea, the crowns, and the creatures.

But the key word, the concept at the very center, is actually the word *throne*. It's central to the entire Book of Revelation. If the various doorways symbolize the journey, the throne gives us the final destination. The word is found forty-six times throughout Revelation. It speaks of sovereignty, reign, and order. It reminds us that, amidst all the chaos of earth, there is absolute Kingship in heaven.

Our Lord still rules; He has never vacated that throne. With all that John sees and all of his marveling, the central image is that throne and the fact that it is not vacant. If we took with us always the image of the Lord on His throne, we would never panic. We would never give in to anxiety or despair. We may think the inmates are running the asylum here on earth, but God is still sovereign.

DAZZLING IMAGERY

We notice one other intriguing item. Amidst all the description—of the many-eyed creatures, of the white-garbed elders, of the glittering crystal sea—there is no description of Him who sits on the throne. We know from the full counsel of Scripture that no mortal has beheld God and lived. Moses had to peek from the obscured angle of a cave wall to catch a fleeting image of the passing glory of God. Here, John cannot describe for us the appearance of the King in his vision. God is always described in purely symbolic terminology, lest we be tempted to create images of Him and compromise His holiness and perfection, which is far beyond our grasp. We cannot worship that which fits comfortably in our conceptions.

So John cannot tell us how God appeared in any literal sense, for there is no literal sense within human capabilities of perception. But he can tell us, in an indirect way, that He was "like a jasper and a sardius stone in appearance" (Revelation 4:3a).

Why would John come up with such a comparison? What he called "jasper" would be, in our modern approximation, a diamond—dazzlingly beautiful, many faceted, projecting its glittering shards of light to dance across the great walls. The other stone, called "sardius," was what we would call a ruby. It was named for the town near which such a stone had been found. The ruby is fiery and bright, complementing the dazzling white of the diamond's projection.

These images would be considered rich poetry by any human reckoning, but they're merely crude symbols of the magnificence that John beheld. Limited by our humanity, we can't imagine anything much more majestic than the finest stones compressed over countless eons within the earth. Thus John beheld perfect fire and white radiance emanating from the throne and the person of God, and these are his words—the Holy Spirit's words—to help us gaze in a mirror dimly and try to understand.

Then we come to the wonderful rainbow, "in appearance like an emerald," which was all around the throne. Again, John borrows from the imagery of precious jewelry. We have the fiery red of the ruby, the dazzling dance of the diamond, and the eternal green beauty of the emerald, perhaps suggesting that in His presence, around His throne, new life is green, now and forever.

The rainbow encircled the throne. It was an unbroken circle, unlike the semicircular rainbows we see on a rainy day. In heaven, all is complete, unbroken, eternal. John would have thought of the covenant between God and His people. The rainbow had spoken the permanence of God's promise since Noah's family stepped off the ark. In the Old Testament, God gave the rainbow to Noah in the aftermath of the first judgment. I can't help but speculate that for John, the rainbow served as the prelude to the final judgment. The rainbow might be a reminder to John (and to us) that, amidst all the terrifying things set to happen as earth's final destiny played out, God would still occupy His throne. The Lord, the King, would still rule with a sure hand. He would be, once and forever, the keeper of promises.

Of Kings and Creatures

John saw the throne, the fiery ruby radiance, the white light, and the eternal emerald purity. He saw the elegance of the rainbow emanating from the throne. Then, as his perception took in more of the surroundings, he perceived the lesser thrones. And there he saw the twenty-four elders.

All through the years, these elders have kept scholars busy speculating about their identity. Who were these men who kept company with the Alpha and Omega in the great throne room? I believe a careful reading leads to the conclusion that they represent the church of the living God, the family of the King. The next chapter of Revelation offers a fairly clear identification of the elders:

> Now when He had taken the scroll, the four living creatures and
> the twenty-four elders fell down before the Lamb, each having a
> harp, and golden bowls full of incense, which are the prayers of
> the saints. And they sang a new song, saying:
> "You are worthy to take the scroll,
> And to open its seals;
> For You were slain,
> And have redeemed us to God by Your blood
> Out of every tribe and tongue and people and nation,
> And have made us kings and priests to our God;
> And we shall reign on the earth."
>
> —REVELATION 5:8–10

Their song in particular tells us who the elders are. They come "out of every tribe and tongue and people and nation," and they have been redeemed and set to rule. The twenty-four elders are the church of the living God—you and me.

But what do we make of the beasts? John tells us of these wonderful, terrifying creatures with six wings and six eyes, fashioned after men and the greatest of earthly creatures. And they're totally given to praise and worship of our holy God. John sees and hears the elders and the creatures, falling down before Him in a scene of fiery magnificence. We desperately need to take in that imagery ourselves. Silly movies and television shows have depicted folks in the next life wearing choir robes and feathery wings, perched on clouds and singing hymns. We begin to murmur about how dull it must be up there. Do we really want to spend eternity strumming a harp and itching within our robes?

I need not tell you there's no scriptural basis for such a mundane conception. We need to cast out the cartoon and reclaim the fiery image, given in Revelation of what it's like to stand in the presence of the dazzling throne, falling upon our knees in the shallows of the glassy sea, with the rainbow radiance of God, far beyond diamond and ruby and emerald, piercing us—not blinding us, but giving us true and ultimate vision. We'll sing then through tears of joy and find that all around us our kindred souls are joining in the song. Perfect harmony, knit together by every strand of cultural and social and temporal difference, will rise from the hearts and lungs of that celestial choir.

The song will be magnificent! Through a window, we'll see the earth, the skies, and the weary years pass into twilight and then dust. And we'll be left in the presence of the King forevermore, and there will be no more tears but the pure, crystal tears of eternal joy.

Holy, holy, holy! Lord God Almighty!
Early in the morning our song shall rise to Thee;
Holy, holy, holy, merciful and mighty!
God in three Persons, blessed Trinity!

Holy, holy, holy! all the saints adore Thee,
Casting down their golden crowns around the glassy sea;
Cherubim and seraphim falling down before Thee,
Who wert, and art, and evermore shalt be.

Holy, holy, holy! tho' the darkness hide Thee,
Tho' the eye of sinful man Thy glory may not see;
Only Thou art holy; there is none beside Thee,
Perfect in pow'r, in love, and purity.

Holy, holy, holy! Lord God Almighty!
All Thy works shall praise Thy name,
 in earth, and sky, and sea;
Holy, holy, holy; merciful and mighty!
God in three Persons, blessed Trinity![3]

15

Eternal Perspective

FIFTEEN

Eternal Perspective

P AUL AZINGER was at the top of his profession, and that profession was a pretty desirable one: PGA golfer. But at the age of thirty-three, he faced his greatest crisis. He was diagnosed with cancer.

I know exactly how he felt. When all had seemed so calm in my life, when my ministry truly seemed fruitful, I faced that same terrifying prospect. I've told that story in greater detail in another book, *A Bend in the Road*.[1]

Azinger had just won a PGA championship and held the championship trophies from ten PGA tournaments. Why now? Why this? He wrote:

> A genuine feeling of fear came over me. I could die from cancer. Then another reality hit me even harder. I'm going to die eventually anyway, whether from cancer or something else. It's just a question of when. Everything I had accomplished in golf became meaningless to me. All I wanted to do was live.[2]

Azinger had a close friend named Larry Moody, who was leading a Bible study for golfers on the tour. Moody had made a statement that completely changed Azinger's paradigm of life and death. He had said, "Zinger, we're not in the land of the living and heading for the land of the dying. We're in the land of the dying trying to get to the land of the living."

Paul Azinger had never thought of it that way. Not even close. Moody's statement caused him to rethink his entire approach to life as he submitted to chemotherapy, worked through his recovery, and eventually returned to the PGA tour. Soon he was playing golf again, just as he had before. But his perspective was no longer a temporal one. He wrote:

> I've made a lot of money since I've been on the tour, and I've won a lot of tournaments, but that happiness is always temporary. The only way you will ever have true contentment is in a personal relationship with Jesus Christ. I'm not saying that nothing ever bothers me and I don't have problems, but I feel like I've found the answer to the six-foot hole.[3]

Most of us live under the enduring illusion that this earth, so filled with pain, is the land of the living. We know it's not much, but it's home after all. On the other hand, we don't know about that next world. It's cloaked in mystery.

But we should know. We devote our lives to studying God's Word, worshiping Him, and anticipating eternity in His presence. This life is only a brief prelude, a puny grain of sand compared to the vast, infinite seashore of eternity. It's important how we live today, but why should we fear the final, glorious culmination of which this life only hints? I had my own bout with a life-threatening disease, and I'm none too eager to leave the ministry God has given me here. But I have a deeper appreciation, and a more eager anticipation, of the joys still in store. Now, having looked into the face of eternity through so many anxious moments, I feel that I'm better able to possess that frame of mind that enables us to superimpose God's outlook on the moment's details.

It's called an eternal perspective, and it's the very key to worshiping God in every moment of your daily life.

Escape from Exile

Let's return for a moment to our old friend, John the Apostle, who stood with us at the doorway to eternity. It's interesting to think about his later life, after Jesus had ascended to His Father.

John was part of the inner circle of disciples, one whom Jesus often called for special tasks. John was present at Gethsemane. He was there, while most of the disciples hid, at the foot of the cross, where Jesus asked him to care for His mother. It was John who beat Peter in a footrace to the empty tomb. The "beloved disciple" is often depicted as gentle and warm, but actually Jesus gave John and his brother, James, the title "Sons of Thunder."

And why not? John stood witness to the awesome vision at the Mount of Transfiguration. He stood and watched Jesus ascend into heaven. But John, and John alone, was invited to view the great scene of praise and worship in the throne room, as we've detailed in the preceding chapter. Indeed he saw the lightning and heard the thunder that proceeded from the great throne of the Almighty.

But John's life involved much heartbreak. He was exiled to the island of Patmos, cut off from his friends during such a crisis in the history of the young church. From day to day he had to wonder whether his friends still lived, or whether the Roman emperor Domitian had captured and executed them. Jesus had lived and died and bled for His church, and now it was under daily attack by the empire. This, too, brought John pain. Nor did he have any illusions about what faced him down the road. Early on, Jesus had told John and his brother that they would drink from the same cup He was destined to sip. He clearly meant martyrdom. In the meantime, John faced the simple but significant trials of aging.

John may have been the last disciple still alive, but he faced a daily existence of increased feebleness and painful exile, even as he watched his friends succumb so violently to the persecution of the young church.

So John waited out his life in exile. All of us do that in a certain way; Paul described us as citizens of another world, aliens and strangers in this one. We're all exiles in that sense, but I'm certain John felt his alienation keenly, more and more with each passing day. He had borne witness to the tragedy of crucifixion and the triumph of resurrection, but now, in his solitude, the world seemed dim indeed—until one day the door of heaven swung open.

Suddenly the light of heaven pierced through a crack in a door that hadn't been there a moment ago. And the voice told him he would be allowed to enter, "to boldly go where no man had gone before." He would stand at the threshold of eternity to record what he saw, so countless generations yet unborn could vicariously glimpse the same wonders through his eyes.

One moment, the elderly John might well have been lamenting his rheumatism. He might have felt the aches in his joints, or he might have been tossing and turning through another restless night. His thoughts may have been on absent friends, on trial or in prison. Perhaps he was reliving the wonderful days of Jesus' physical presence and wishing that time hadn't come and gone so quickly. If he was anything like you and me, John was immersed in the disappointments of this world, the land of the dead. And then, when the door was suddenly thrown open, John walked through the portal to an eternal perspective.

The View from On High

In these chapters we've attempted, through the lamentable limits of my writing ability, to stand there with John. We've challenged you to capture with your imagination the sights John was allowed to see, for that's why they're recorded in the Bible. The Lamb bids us to come and worship. He wants us to stand before His throne and sing praises, to experience the liberation that comes when a divine perspective takes root within us.

John, we must assume, was never again the same. Like Paul Azinger and countless others, an incredible moment of personal revelation showed him the difference between the land of the living and the land of the dead, and it made all the difference. We need not live with the dust of death always ruling our senses. If we can only learn to worship, to cast our earthly crowns before Him and exalt Him in all that we do, we'll bring a bit of eternity back into the land of the dead. We'll find new vigor, new encouragement, and new joy to face the everyday situations of life.

The great work of humanity is one of worship and praise, but that doesn't imply an abandonment of normal life and work; it transforms them to something entirely new. Having dwelt even for a moment in the company of the King, we're bathed in an eternal perspective. "The things of earth will grow strangely dim," as the hymn says, "in the light of His glory and grace." That light washes over everything and shows it to us with new illumination. Your occupation will seem brand-new; you'll work better and more effectively, but it will no longer rule your life. You'll function more lovingly in family life, but you won't be dominated by its pressures. You'll be a better friend, a better citizen, and a more fruitful child of God's kingdom.

When you attain that perspective, you'll begin to be aware of the infinite difference between the eternal and the temporal. Temporal matters weigh us down, but in the light of eternity they're small indeed. In C. S. Lewis's allegory *The Great Divorce,* a character experiences his own version of the experience that John had at the gates of heaven. This man rides a bus to paradise and finds that it's a land that is more fully, powerfully real than any place he could have imagined. It is a land where everything is bright, gigantic, bursting with color, and expressed in its fullest implications. But hell, he discovers, is no more than a fleck of dust in comparison. It is tiny, for hell is constantly concerned with littleness. It constantly folds in upon itself and becomes smaller, even as it takes in hapless souls.[4] In the same way, our lives become smaller and more confined when we're taken in by the world and its deceptions. There is less color. There is no joy at all.

As we read Revelation 4, on the other hand, we're struck by the brightness, by the color, by the gigantic proportions of all that John allows us to glimpse. We can only wonder, then worship. Suddenly everything in this world—everything not part of God's eternal purposes—seems small and pitiable in contrast, not worthy of our interest.

Perhaps you've stood at the highest point of the Rocky Mountains or at the crest of the Grand Canyon and found yourself unable to speak. It's healthy to take in the larger perspective. We live our lives, more and more, in little cubicles. We think small thoughts and indulge in small pleasures. Yet God wants so much more for us. He wants us to find the ultimate joy that is attainable only through an eternal perspective. One of the truly wonderful by-products of worship is that life becomes expansive and beautiful again. It's like the Christmas you lost when you stopped being a child. Worship God with all your heart, and you'll be a child again.

It sounds great. But how can we make it happen?

SET ON ETERNITY

Paul tells us in Colossians 3:1–2, to set our minds on eternal things, not earthly ones. After all, he says, we have been raised with Christ. Our spirits dwell with Him in the heavenly places; why should we become comfortable in the gutter? In that very passage, Paul refers to Christ's sitting at the right hand of the Father. That, he says, is what we are to set our minds upon. Again, the idea is for us to kneel before the eternal throne, just as John did.

All of this sounds high-minded and pious, but how do we break it down to practical, human terms? We still have jobs to attend to, children to feed, spouses to please, and homes to maintain. We live in a real world with real problems.

That's precisely why we must learn to worship as an everyday lifestyle. Even if we took part in wonderful, powerful worship once a week from a church pew, it wouldn't be enough. The Spirit of God accompanies us everywhere we go, and we can worship Him in the very midst of daily life. The list I'm going to offer you here is a very practical one, but not an exhaustive one. These are ideas to jump-start your praise life, and I recommend that you select a few and put them to immediate use.

- ***Praise God through music.*** I've mentioned in a previous chapter just how much I depend on godly music of worship and praise. Let me recommend that you find a cassette tape or CD that really seems to touch you and to take you into God's presence—then stick with that one for at least a week. There's plenty of good praise music out there, but my suggestion is for you to choose one recording of songs and really spend some time with it, digging deeply into the words and praising God through them. After a while, you'll know those words and you'll be able to sing along even when you're away from your stereo. This is wonderful for commuting in traffic. Wouldn't you like to see what rush hour would be like if everyone were praising God as they drove?

- **Praise God through Scripture memory.** I can hear you groaning—stop that! I can commend to you no task more worthy of your time than learning the great Bible verses by memory—"by heart," as we used to say. For once those verses are imbedded in your heart, they've become a permanent part of you. You've given the Holy Spirit a tool for encouragement in your life. He'll bring you to recall those verses just when you need them. But in this context, I'm recommending that you memorize passages such as Revelation 4 or Psalm 100 so that, as you lie in the dark or scrub in the shower, you can use them to praise God wherever you may be. I've read stories of prisoners of war who struggled to recall and then share with each other every Bible verse they could remember from childhood. They had no Bibles, but no one could take their memories from them. The Word of God had become a part of them, and it sustained them through their suffering. Feed your mind and soul with the everlasting Word.

- **Praise God in daily intervals.** Most of us are familiar with the idea of a daily quiet time or morning devotions. These times are essential for every Christian, but your goal is to praise and worship all through the day, not simply during a morning time segment. Set times when you know you'll be able to stop and whisper your praises to God or to sing them in your mind or even full voice. For example, you might decide you'll praise God each morning in the shower, during devotions, at the beginning of your morning coffee break, just before lunch, in rush-hour traffic, and just before you climb into bed at night. Begin with three or more of these and make a firm covenant to stop and praise God at these appointed times. Carry a pocket New Testament or even some note cards with favorite verses. After a while, it won't happen only at preset intervals. You'll be worshiping on the go constantly.

- *Praise God through visual reminders.* We all need a few personal billboards in life. Sometimes they take the form of refrigerator magnets or coffee mugs. These bear little sayings and reminders about dieting or being the "World's Greatest Mom." I challenge you to see how many worship reminders you can insert into your daily field of vision. Don't do this in a way that would be obnoxious to your coworkers at the office. But keep a note card with your current memory verse or a favorite psalm taped to your computer terminal. Put a reminder on the refrigerator (and remove the other ones that might detract). The bathroom mirror is a good place. So is the dashboard of your car. Every time you see one of these, you'll be reminded to stop and offer exaltation and thanksgiving to your God.

- *Praise God through a small group.* Talk to some like-minded friends who share your desire to be more devoted to worship. Gather with them once a week, at a convenient time, to focus on praise and worship together. Most of the time we emphasize Bible study in these groups, and that's fine. We need to be doing that, too, of course. But perhaps your group can take a period of time to reorient yourselves a bit more in the direction of worship. If you work in an office, you might find a partner or small group of believers who will meet you fifteen minutes before work each day to praise God together.

197

I guarantee you that if you'll try at least one or two of these initiatives, your life will be changed. Your anxiety will melt away. You'll be worshiping gladly, and you'll begin to be conformed to the image of Christ.

The Company You Keep

I heard about an old man who worked in the evenings, cleaning an office building. Jim, an executive, would often work until after dark, and he'd catch a glimpse of the old-timer arriving with his mops, his brooms—and an infectious smile.

Jim was under a great deal of stress. He was putting in countless hours, but he couldn't seem to climb the executive ladder with the speed he desired. He was becoming moody and often depressed. One evening, when there was no one in the building but himself and the old man, he paused to watch as the janitor headed for the bathroom to perform the usual cleaning rituals. Jim shook his head derisively. "I don't see how you can derive so much enjoyment from scrubbing a latrine," he said. "What would it take to drive that smile off your face?"

The janitor actually laughed; he wasn't offended. "Never thought about that question, sir," he said. "I used to have some jobs that were prettier ones, I guess. I drove me a truck. Good pay, lots of hours talking to Jesus. But times were bad, and I lost that job. After that I worked in the public park, and I liked that, too. Plenty of sunshine. Best of all, when I took that job, Jesus came with me. I could talk things over with Him while I raked the leaves and picked up the litter. That was nice. But that job didn't last, either."

"Life is tough, isn't it?" said Jim, nodding his head. "You have to admit it's given you a raw deal."

"Oh, I don't know about that," said the janitor with a faraway smile.

"I'm indoors now, and that's nice when it rains. It's dark and lonely sometimes, but Jesus is there whenever I call for Him. He would never leave me nor forsake me, know what I mean? I don't know, maybe I'd feel differently about cleaning a toilet if the Lord Jesus didn't stay by my side. He walks with me and He talks with me, and the whole time, sir, I'm actually getting paid! The way I look at it, why shouldn't I be smiling?"

In beautiful words we paraphrased earlier, the poet Elizabeth Barrett Browning said:

> Earth's crammed with heaven,
>
> And every common bush afire with God;
>
> But only he who sees, takes off his shoes,
>
> The rest sit round it and pluck blackberries.[5]

I don't know what you see in the bushes around you—the consuming fire of heaven or mere blackberries. It's a question of whether you have eternal perspective. Wherever you go, whatever you do, the Lord Jesus longs to be your constant companion. You have the opportunity to praise and worship Him all through the day. He once washed the dirty feet of His disciples, so the details of your job make no difference.

If you will only practice His presence, you will find an eternal perspective taking root in your soul. You will begin to see this world though heavenly eyes. The trials will seem more trivial, and the blessings will be more obvious to you. You'll see every person as Christ sees him or her, and don't be surprised if you find yourself washing a foot or two, in time.

Wherever you go will be a fine place to be. And whatever you do will be filled with an irrepressible joy, because you're in the company of the King.

16

I Wonder As I Wander

SIXTEEN

∽ *I Wonder As I Wander* ∽

WHAT A JOURNEY we've enjoyed together—yet it's only been the first tentative step down a long path that will lead you joyfully through this life and on into the next. It's certainly a step in the right direction.

As you wander through this world, I pray that you'll experience the wonder of worship every moment of every day. In the beginning, you'll find it to be a discipline like any other. There may be more willpower than joy at times. You may sometimes feel awkward and uncomfortable, and find yourself saying, "Is all this really true? I don't *see* anything in it. I don't *hear* God's voice. I don't *feel* His presence." There are days like that for all of us.

The pursuit of God has no shortcuts. You simply must keep walking, keep seeking, and keep yearning. Keep at it, and you won't be disappointed. Listen for His words gently whispered in your ear: "I love those who love me, and those who seek me diligently will find me" (Proverbs 8:17). He has also given you this promise: "Then you will call upon Me and go and pray to Me, and I will listen to you. And you will seek Me and find Me, when you search for Me with all your heart" (Jeremiah 29:12–13).

If you're serious about this new way of life, if you'll settle for nothing less than living each moment in the wonder of worship, then that's exactly what it's going to take: searching for God with all your heart. I assure you He isn't hiding; you can look for Him in all the old familiar places. Review His great works in the lives of others, and relive the great wonders He has performed in your own life. Stop to smell the roses, as they say, and remind yourself who it was who designed every flower. Stop to take in a few more sunsets, and look a bit more closely to see the presence of God in the lives of others.

Seek Him anywhere and everywhere. In time, you'll cultivate the sacred art of meeting Him at every crossroad, of feeling His breath in every wind—the art we've referred to as eternal perspective. When the road dips into the valley, there you'll know His hand of comfort. When the road climbs to a glorious peak, there you'll celebrate His hand of power. Through pain and victory, each new step will help you come to know Him better.

And then you'll *wonder.* You'll wander through the wilderness of this life, and you'll wonder at the sheer magnificence of your God, at its glorious height and depth and breadth whose measurements are infinite. And here is the paradox: The larger He grows in your estimation, the more you will feel—little? Not exactly. *Loved* is closer to it. For God is love, and coming to know Him better, coming to worship Him more constantly, means becoming more and more immersed in that love. Make worship the guiding light of your very existence, the goal of your life mission, and you will know love as you've never known it.

And what happens to those who are more loved? They overflow from the outpouring. They drench their surroundings with love. All those around you will feel it. God will love you with a love that molds you, sculpts you, and shapes you into a new creature who resembles Christ more with every passing day. You'll love people—all people—as Christ loves them. You'll even love yourself more deeply, more appropriately, because God loves you.

What more can I tell you about the wonders that lie before you as you wander down the road of daily worship? By now, you should be ready to stop hearing and start tasting. Today is the first day of the rest of your life. What do you have planned for the next hour? The next day? The next week? Whatever plans you may have, they are opportunities for worship. So let's worship together, each moment. Today or tomorrow, wherever you are when you stop to praise the name of your Lord, the likelihood is that I'll be praising God with you—along with countless Christians across the world, lifting up a worldwide harmony of praise that is delightful to His ears. And if enough of us join the chorus, what miracles might return to this world?

> O Worship the King, all glorious above,
> And gratefully sing His wonderful love;
> Our Shield and Defender, the Ancient of Days,
> Pavilioned in splendor, and girded with praise.
>
> O tell of His might, O Sing of His grace,
> Whose robe is the light, whose canopy space!
> His chariots of wrath the deep thunderclouds form,
> And dark is His path on the wings of the storm.
>
> Thy bountiful care, what tongue can recite?

My Heart's Desire

It breathes in the air, it shines in the light,
It streams from the hills, it descends to the plain,
And sweetly distills in the dew and the rain.

Frail children of dust, and feeble as frail,
In Thee do we trust, nor find Thee to fail:
Thy mercies how tender, how firm to the end,
Our Maker, Defender, Redeemer, and Friend.[1]

~ ENDNOTES ~

CHAPTER 2: DO YOU EVER WONDER?

1. Bill Moyers, *A World of Ideas II,* PBS video, quoted in Freeman, Rusty, "Night of Wonder," *Journal for Preachers,* Advent 2000, 11.
2. Albert Einstein, quoted in S. M. Ulam, *Adventures of a Mathematician* (New York: Charles Scribner's Sons, 1976), 289.

CHAPTER 3: WHERE A KING MAKES HIS HOME

1. Source unknown.
2. C. S. Lewis, *Reflections on the Psalms* (New York: Harcourt, Brace, & Jovanovich, 1958), 90, 93.

CHAPTER 4: A TEMPLE ON WHEELS

1. Robert Boyd Munger, *My Heart—Christ's Home* (Downer's Grove, Ill.: InterVarsity Press, 1986).

2. C. S. Lewis, *The Screwtape Letters,* revised ed. (New York: Macmillan, 1982), 38–39.

Chapter 6: All or Nothing at All

1. Robert E. Webber, *Worship Is a Verb* (Peabody, Mass.: Hendrickson Publishers, 1992).

Chapter 7: This Hallowed Ground

1. Story adapted from Norman Grubb, *C. T. Studd: Cricketer and Pioneer* (Ft. Washington, Penn.: Christian Literature Crusade, 1982), 46.

Chapter 8: The Language of Angels

1. F. Olin Stockwell, *Meditations from a Prison Cell* (Nashville: Upper Room, 1954), quoted in Kenneth W. Osbeck, *The Endless Song* (Grand Rapids, Mich.: Kregel, 1987), 18.
2. Andrew Fletcher, quoted in Michael Coleman and Ed Lindquist, *Come and Worship* (Old Tappen, N.J.: Chosen Books, 1989), 26.

Chapter 9: Let Heaven and Nature Sing

1. "Our Daily Bread," June 14, 1996.
2. John Wesley, *Select Hymns* (n.p., 1761), introduction.
3. Quoted in Sammy Tippit, *Worthy of Worship* (Chicago: Moody, 1989), 90.

4. Ira Sankey biography, found at www.swordoftheLord.com/biography.asp.

5. John Piper, *The Hidden Smile of God* (Wheaton, Ill.: Crossway Books, 2001), 93–94.

6. Lindsay Terry, "A Song Written for One Family," *The Communicator,* December 2001.

CHAPTER 10: THIS MEANS WAR!

1. Story adapted from Michael Coleman and Ed Linquist, *Come and Worship* (Old Tappan, N.J.: Chosen Books, 1989), 74–76.

2. Donald E. Demaray, *Alive to God Through Prayer* (Grand Rapids: Baker Book House, 1965), 27.

3. Jack R. Taylor, *The Hallelujah Factor* (Nashville: Broadman, 1983), 31.

4. St. Ignatius of Loyola, *The Epistle to the Ephesians,* Chapter XIII, lines 93–94.

CHAPTER 11: STRANGE BUT TRUE WORSHIP STORIES

1. Michael Coleman and Ed Linquist, *Come and Worship* (Old Tappan, N.J.: Chosen Books, 1989), 80–83.

CHAPTER 12: WORSHIP IN THE DARK

1. "The Solid Rock," words by Edward Mote (1797–1874).

Chapter 13: Knowledge and Trust

1. Bruce Larson, *Wind and Fire,* quoted in Hewett, James S., Ed., *Illustrations Unlimited* (Wheaton, IL: Tyndale, 1988), 189.
2. Joseph S. Carroll, *How to Worship Jesus Christ* (Chicago: Moody Press, 1984), 57–58.

Chapter 14: At the Door of Eternity

1. Edward K. Rowell, ed., *Quotes and Idea Starters for Preaching and Teaching* (Grand Rapids, Mich.: Baker Books, 2000), 183.
2. Leslie B. Flynn, *Worship: Together We Celebrate* (Wheaton, Ill.: Victor Books, 1983), 11.
3. "Holy, Holy, Holy," words by Reginald Heber (1783–1826).

Chapter 15: Eternal Perspective

1. David Jeremiah, *A Bend in the Road* (Nashville: Word Publishing, 2000).
2. Robert Russell, "Resurrection Promises," Preaching Today (Tape 151).
3. Ibid.
4. C. S. Lewis, *The Great Divorce* (New York: Macmillan, 1946).
5. Elizabeth Barrett Browning, "Aurora Leigh," no. 86, lines 61–64, quoted in Nicholson & Lee, eds., *The Oxford Book of English Mystical Verse* (London: Oxford, 1917).

Chapter 16: I Wonder As I Wander

1. "O Worship the King," words by Robert Grant (1779–1838).